Classic American Love Poems

Love Poetry from Hippocrene Books...

Classic American Love Poems
Classic English Love Poems
Classic French Love Poems
Hebrew Love Poems
Irish Love Poems: Dánta Grá
Scottish Love Poems: A Personal Anthology
Longing for a Kiss: Love Poems from Many Lands
Love Poems from Around the World
Treasury of Wedding Poems, Quotations & Short Stories

Love Quotations & Proverbs
Treasury of Love Quotations from Many Lands
Treasury of Love Proverbs from Many Lands

Classic American Love Poems

~

THE EDITORS OF HIPPOCRENE BOOKS

ILLUSTRATED BY

ROSEMARY FOX

HIPPOCRENE BOOKS, INC.
New York

Acknowledgments

"The Voice", copyright © 1955 by Theodore Roethke. From THE COLLECTED POEMS OF THEODORE ROETHKE by Theodore Roethke. Used by permission of Doubleday, a division of Bantam Doubleday Dell Publishing Group, Inc.

"Restatement of Romance" from COLLECTED POEMS by Wallace Stevens. Copyright © 1936 by Wallace Stevens and renewed by Holly Stevens. Reprinted by permission of Alfred A. Knopf, Inc.

"Juke Box Love Song" from COLLECTED POEMS by Langston Hughes. Copyright © 1994 by the estate of Langston Hughes. Reprinted by permission of Alfred A. Knopf, Inc.

"Remembrance" and "Refusal" from AND STILL I RISE by Maya Angelou. Copyright © 1978 by Maya Angelou. Reprinted by permission of Random House, Inc.

"The Maid's Thought" from COLLECTED POETRY OF ROBINSON JEFFERS by Robinson Jeffers. Copyright © 1924 and renewed 1952 by Robinson Jeffers. Reprinted by permission of Random House, Inc.

"Love Letter" from CROSSING THE WATER by Sylvia Plath. Copyright © 1962 by Ted Hughes. Reprinted by permission of HarperCollins Publishers, Inc.

Reprinted by permission of Farrar, Straus & Giroux, Inc.:
"Ah when you drift hover before you kiss", and "Your shining—where?—rays my wide room with gold" from COLLECTED POEMS 1937-1971 by John Berryman. Copyright © 1989 by Kate Donahue Berryman. "Insomnia", "Letter to N.Y." from THE COMPLETE POEMS 1927-1979 by Elizabeth Bishop. Copyright © 1979, 1983 by Alice Helen Methfessel. "Men Loved Wholly Beyond Wisdom" from THE BLUE ESTUARIES: POEMS 1923-1968 by Louise Bogan. Copyright © 1968 by Louise Bogan. Copyright renewed © 1996 by Ruth Limmer.

Reprinted by permission of Hill and Wang, a division of Farrar, Straus & Giroux, Inc.:
"Private Worship" from COLLECTED AND NEW POEMS 1924-1963 by Mark Van Doren. Copyright © 1963 by Mark Van Doren. Copyright renewed © 1991 by Dorothy G. Van Doren.

For information, address:
HIPPOCRENE BOOKS, INC.
171 Madison Avenue
New York, NY 10016

ISBN 0-7818-0894-4

Cover art by John Singer Sargent.

Printed in the United States of America.

Contents

Preface

The American poetic tradition, while relatively new compared to those of Europe, the Middle East and the Far East, has still thrived and left an indelible mark on world literature. This volume celebrates the love lyrics of American poets from colonial days to the twentieth century. The anthology begins with seventeenth-century Puritan poet, Anne Bradstreet, whose bittersweet verses chronicle the everyday trials of domestic life, religious beliefs and family tragedies in tender yet beautiful lines. It also includes Edgar Allan Poe's haunting elegies to lost love, Emily Dickinson's concise but powerful stanzas, Walt Whitman's verses celebrating sensuality, freedom and the American spirit, and works by the giants of modern American poetry—Wallace Stevens, William Carlos Williams and Ezra Pound. There are also verses from African-American poets, Gwendolyn Brooks, James Baldwin and Maya Angelou, who describe love, loss and the black experience in America.

These poems address the many and varied facets of love with all of its joys and heartbreaks—romantic love, familial and brotherly love, love of nature and love of country. As a new century opens before us, it is appropriate to look again at the inspiring love poems of great poets and writers, both of our age and of previous centuries, who transformed conventional styles and forms to forge a unique American poetic voice through their art.

ANNE BRADSTREET (1612?–1672)

A Letter to Her Husband, Absent Upon Publick Employment

My head, my heart, mine Eyes, my life, nay more,
My joy, my Magazine of earthly store,
If two be one, as surely thou and I,
How stayest thou there, whilst I at *Ipswich* lye?
So many steps, head from the heart to sever
If but a neck, soon should we be together:
I like the earth this season, mourn in black,
My Sun is gone so far in's Zodiack,
Whom whilst I 'joy'd, nor storms, nor frosts I felt,
His warmth such frigid colds did cause to melt.
My chilled limbs now nummed lye forlorn;
Return, return sweet *Sol* from *Capricorn*;
In this dead time, alas what can I more
Then view those fruits which through thy heat I bore?
Which sweet contentment yield me for a space,
True living Pictures of their Fathers face.
O strange effect! Now thou art *Southward* gone,
I weary grow, the tedious day so long;
But when thou *Northward* to me shalt return,
I wish my Sun may never set, but burn
Within the Cancer of my glowing breast,
The welcome house of him my dearest guest.
Where ever, ever stay, and go not thence,
Till natures sad decree shall call thee hence;
Flesh of thy flesh, bone of thy bone,
I here, thou there, yet both but one.

Before the Birth of One of Her Children

All things within this fading world hath end,
Adversity doth still our joyes attend;
No tyes so strong, no friends so clear and sweet,
But with deaths parting blow is sure to meet.
The sentence past is more irrevocable;
A common thing, yet oh inevitable;
How soon, my Dear, death may my steps attend,
How soon't may be thy Lot to lose thy friend,
We both are ignorant, yet love bids me
These farewell lines to recommend to thee,
That when that knot's unty'd that made us one,
I may seem thine, who in effect am none.
And if I see not half my dayes that's due,
What nature would, God grant to yours and you;
The many faults that well you know I have,
Let be interr'd in my oblivious grave;
If any worth or virtue were in me,
Let that live freshly in thy memory
And when thou feel'st no grief, as I no harms,
Yet love thy dead, who long lay in thine arms:
And when thy loss shall be repaid with gains
Look to my little babes my dear remains.
And if thou love thy self, or loved'st me
These O protect from step Dames injury.
And if chance to thine eyes shall bring this verse,
With some sad sighs honour my absent Herse;
And kiss this paper for thy loves dear sake,
Who with salt tears this last Farewel did take.

To My Dear and Loving Husband

If ever two were one, then surely we.
If ever man were lov'd by wife, then thee;
If ever wife was happy in a man,
Compare with me ye women if you can.
I prize thy love more than whole Mines of gold,
Or all the riches that the East doth hold.
My love is such that Rivers cannot quench,
Nor ought but love from thee, give recompence.
Thy love is such I can no way repay,
The heavens reward thee manifold I pray.
Then while we live, in love lets so persever,
That when we live no more, we may live ever.

PHILLIS WHEATLEY (1753?–1784)

To a Lady on the Death of Her Husband

GRIM monarch! See, depriv'd of vital breath,
A young physician in the dust of death:
Dost thou go on incessant to destroy,
Our griefs to double, and lay waste our joy?
Enough thou never yet wast known to say,
Though millions die, the vassals of thy sway:
Nor youth, nor science, nor the ties of love,
Nor ought on earth thy flinty heart can move.
The friend, the spouse from his dire dart to save,
In vain we ask the sovereign of the grave.
Fair mourner, there see thy lov'd *Leonard* laid,
And o'er him spread the deep impervious shade;
Clos'd are his eyes, and heavy fetters keep
His senses bound in never-waking sleep,
Till time shall cease, till many a starry world
Shall fall from heav'n, in dire confusion hurl'd,
Till nature in her final wreck shall lie,
And her last groan shall rend the azure sky:
Not, not till then his active soul shall claim
His body, a divine immortal frame.

But see the softly-stealing tears apace
Pursue each other down the mourner's face;
But cease thy tears, bid ev'ry sigh depart,
And cast the load of anguish from thine heart:
From the cold shell of his great soul arise,
And look beyond, thou native of the skies;
There fix thy view, where fleeter than the wind
Thy *Leonard* mounts; and leaves the earth behind.
Thyself prepare to pass the vale of night
To join for ever on the hills of light:
To thine embrace his joyful spirit moves
To thee, the partner of his earthly loves;
He welcomes thee to pleasures more refin'd,
And better suited to th' immortal mind.

To the Rev. Mr. Pitkin on the Death of His Lady

WHERE Contemplation finds her sacred Spring;
  Where heav'nly Music makes the Centre ring;
  Where Virtue reigns unsulled, and divine;
  Where Wisdom thron'd, and all the Graces shine;
There sits thy Spouse, amid the glitt'ring Throng;
There central Beauty feasts the ravish'd Tongue;
With recent Powers, with recent glories crown'd,
The Choirs angelic shout her Welcome round.
  The virtuous Dead, demand a grateful Tear—
But cease thy Grief a-while, thy Tears forbear,
Not thine alone, the Sorrow I relate,
Thy blooming Off-spring feel the mighty Weight;
Thus, from the Bosom of the tender Vine,
The Branches torn, fall, wither, sink supine.
  Now flies the Soul, tho' Æther unconfin'd.
Thrice happy State of the immortal Mind!
Still in thy Breast tumultuous Passions rise,
And urge the lucent Torrent from thine Eyes.
Amidst the Seats of Heaven, a Place is free
Among those bright angelic Ranks for thee.
For thee, they wait—and with expectant Eye,
Thy Spouse leans forward from th' ethereal Sky,
Thus in my Hearing, "Come away," she cries,
"Partake the sacred Raptures of the Skies!
"Our Bliss divine, to Mortals is unknown,
"And endless Scenes of Happiness our own;
"May the dear Off-spring of our earthly Love,
"Receive Admittance to the Joys above!
"Attune the Harp to more than mortal Lays,
"And pay with us, the Tribute of their Praise
"To Him, who died, dread Justice to appease,
"Which reconcil'd, holds Mercy in Embrace;
"Creation too, her MAKER'S Death bemoan'd,
"Retir'd the Sun, and deep the Centre groan'd.

"He in his Death slew ours, and as he rose,
"He crush'd the Empire of our hated Foes.
"How vain their Hopes to put the GOD to flight,
"And render Vengence to the Sons of Light!"
  Thus having spoke she turn'd away her Eyes,
Which beam'd celestial Radiance o'er the Skies.
Let Grief no longer damp the sacred Fire,
But rise sublime, to equal Bliss aspire;
Thy Sighs no more be wafted by the Wind,
Complain no more, but be to Heav'n resign'd.
'Twas thine to shew those Treasure all divine,
To sooth our Woes, the Task was also thine.
Now Sorrow is recumbent on thy Heart,
Permit the Muse that healing to impart,
Nor can the World, a pitying tear refuse,
They weep, and with them, ev'ry heavenly Muse.

Early Affection

I lov'd thee from the earliest dawn,
  When first I saw thy beauty's ray,
And will, until life's eve comes on,
  And beauty's blossom fades away;
And when all things go well with thee,
With smiles and tears remember me.

I'll love thee when thy morn is past,
  And wheedling gallantry is o'er,
When youth is lost in ages blast,
  And beauty can ascend no more,
And when life's journey ends with thee,
O, then look back and think of me.

I'll love thee with a smile or frown,
  'Mid sorrow's gloom or pleasure's light,
And when the chain of life runs down,
  Pursue thy last eternal flight,
When thou has spread thy wing to flee,
Still, still, a moment wait for me.

I'll love thee for those sparkling eyes,
  To which my fondness was betray'd,
Bearing the tincture of the skies,
  To glow when other beauties fade,
And when they sink too low to see,
Reflect and azure beam on me.

Give All to Love

Give all to love;
Obey thy heart;
Friends, kindred, days,
Estate, good-fame,
Plans, credit and the Muse,—
Nothing refuse.

'Tis a brave master;
Let it have scope:
Follow it utterly,
Hope beyond hope:
High and more high
It dives into noon,
With wing unspent,
Untold intent;
But it is a god,
Knows its own path
And the outlets of the sky.

It was never for the mean;
It requireth courage stout.
Souls above doubt,
Valor unbending,
It will reward,—
They shall return
More than they were,
And ever ascending.

Leave all for love;
Yet, hear me, yet,
One word more thy heart behoved,
One pulse more of firm endeavor,—
Keep thee to-day,
Tomorrow, forever,
Free as an Arab
Of thy beloved.

Cling with life to the maid;
But when the surprise,
First vague shadow of surmise
Flits across her bosom young,
Of a joy apart from thee,
Free be she, fancy-free;
Nor thou detain her vesture's hem,
Nor the palest rose she flung
From her summer diadem.

Though thou loved her as thyself,
As a self of purer clay,
Though her parting dims the day,
Stealing grace from all alive;
Heartily know,
When half-gods go,
The gods arrive.

The Fire of Drift-wood

We sat within the farm-house old,
  Whose windows, looking o'er the bay,
Gave to the sea-breeze damp and cold,
  An easy entrance, night and day.

Not far away we saw the port,
  The strange, old-fashioned, silent town,
The lighthouse, the dismantled fort,
  The wooden houses, quaint and brown.

We sat and talked until the night,
  Descending, filled the little room;
Our faces faded from the sight,
  Our voices only broke the gloom.

We spake of many a vanished scene,
  Of what we once had thought and said,
Of what had been, and might have been,
  And who was changed, and who was dead;

And all that fills the hearts of friends,
  When first they feel, with secret pain,
Their lives thenceforth have separate ends,
  And never can be one again;

The first slight swerving of the heart,
  That words are powerless to express,
And leave it still unsaid in part,
  Or say it in too great excess.

The very tones in which we spake
   Had something strange, I could but mark;
The leaves of memory seemed to make
   A mournful rustling in the dark.

Oft died the words upon our lips,
   As suddenly, from out the fire
Built of the wreck of stranded ships,
   The flames would leap and then expire.

And, as their splendor flashed and failed,
   We thought of wrecks upon the main,
Of ships dismasted, that were hailed
   And sent no answer back again.

The windows, rattling in their frames,
   The ocean, roaring up the beach,
The gusty blast, the bickering flames,
   All mingled vaguely in our speech;

Until they made themselves a part
   Of fancies floating through the brain,
The long-lost ventures of the heart,
   That send no answers back again.

O flames that glowed! O hearts that yearned!
   They were indeed too much akin,
The drift-wood fire without that burned,
   The thoughts that burned and glowed within.

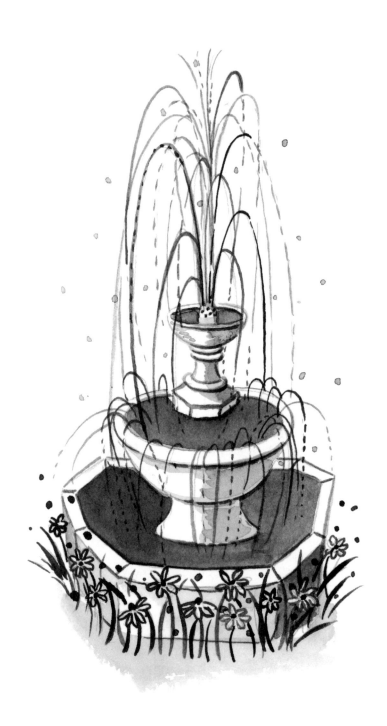

EDGAR ALLAN POE (1809–1849)

To One in Paradise

Thou wast all that to me, love,
  For which my soul did pine—
A green isle in the sea, love,
  A fountain and a shrine,
All wreathed with fairy fruits and flowers,
  And all the flowers were mine.

Ah, dream too bright to last!
  Ah, starry Hope! that didst arise
But to be overcast!
  A voice from out the Future cries,
"On! on!"—but o'er the Past
  (Dim gulf!) my spirit hovering lies
Mute, motionless, aghast!

For, alas! alas! with me
  The light of Life is o'er!
  "No more—no more—no more—"
(Such language holds the solemn sea
  To the sands upon the shore)
Shall bloom the thunder-blasted tree
  Or the stricken eagle soar!

And all my days are trances,
  And all my nightly dreams
Are where thy grey eye glances,
  And where thy footstep gleams—
In what ethereal dances,
  By what eternal streams.

Serenade

So sweet the hour, so calm the time,
I feel it more than half a crime,
When Nature sleeps and stars are mute,
To mar the silence ev'n with lute.
At rest on ocean's brilliant dyes
An image of Elysium lies:
Seven Pleiades entranced in Heaven,
Form in the deep another seven:
Endymion nodding from above
Sees in the sea a second love.
Within the valleys dim and brown,
And on the spectral mountain's crown,
The wearied light is dying down,
And earth, and stars, and sea, and sky
Are redolent of sleep, as I
Am redolent of thee and thine
Enthralling love, my Adeline.

To F—

Beloved! amid the earnest woes
  That crowd around my earthly path—
(Drear path, alas! where grows
Not even one lonely rose)—
  My soul at least a solace hath
In dreams of thee, and therein knows
An Eden of bland repose.

And thus thy memory is to me
  Like some enchanted far-off isle
In some tumultuous sea—
Some ocean throbbing far and free
  With storms—but where meanwhile
Serenest skies continually
  Just o'er that one bright island smile.

Annabel Lee

It was many and many a year ago,
   In a kingdom by the sea,
That a maiden there lived whom you may know
   By the name of Annabel Lee;—
And this maiden she lived with no other thought
   Than to love and be loved by me.

She was a child and I was a child,
   In this kingdom by the sea,
But we loved with a love that was more than a love—
   I and my Annabel Lee—
With a love that the winged seraphs of Heaven
   Coveted her and me.

And this was the reason that, long ago,
   In this kingdom by the sea,
A wind blew out of a cloud, by night
   Chilling my Annabel Lee;
So that her highborn kinsmen came
   And bore her away from me,
To shut her up in a sepulchre
   In this kingdom by the sea.

The angels, not half so happy in Heaven,
   Went envying her and me:
Yes! that was the reason (as all men know,
   In this kingdom by the sea)
That the wind came out of the cloud, chilling
   And killing my Annabel Lee.

But our love it was stronger by far than the love
  Of those who were older than we—
  Of many far wiser than we—
And neither the angels in Heaven above
  Nor the demons down under the sea,
Can ever dissever my soul from the soul
  Of the beautiful Annabel Lee:—

For the moon never beams without bringing me dreams
  Of the beautiful Annabel Lee;
And the stars never rise but I see the bright eyes
  Of the beautiful Annabel Lee;
And so, all the night-tide, I lie down by the side
Of my darling, my darling, my life and my bride,
  In her sepulchre there by the sea—
  In her tomb by the sounding sea.

Song

I saw thee on thy bridal day—
    When a burning blush came o'er thee,
Though happiness around thee lay,
    The world all love before thee:

And in thine eye a kindling light
    (Whatever it might be)
Was all on Earth my aching sight
    Of Loveliness could see.

That blush, perhaps, was maiden shame—
    As such it well may pass—
Though its glow hath raised a fiercer flame
    In the breast of him, alas!

Who saw thee on that bridal day,
    When that deep blush *would* come o'er thee,
Though happiness around thee lay,
    The world all love before thee.

A Dream Within a Dream

Take this kiss upon the brow!
And, in parting from you now,
Thus much let me avow—
You are not wrong, who deem
That my days have been a dream:
Yet if hope has flown away
In a night, or in a day,
In a vision, or in none,
Is it therefore the less *gone*?
All that we see or seem
Is but a dream within a dream.

I stand amid the roar
Of a surf-tormented shore,
And I hold within my hand
Grains of the golden sand—
How few! yet how they creep
Through my fingers to the deep,
While I weep—while I weep!
O God! can I not grasp
Them with a tighter clasp?
O God! can I not save
One from the pitiless wave?
Is *all* that we see or seem
But a dream within a dream?

To Helen

Helen, thy beauty is to me
  Like those Nicaean barks of yore,
That gently, o'er a perfumed sea,
  The weary, wayworn wanderer bore
  To his own native shore.

On desperate seas long wont to roam,
  Thy hyacinth hair, thy classic face,
Thy Naiad airs, have brought me home
  To the glory that was Greece
  And the grandeur that was
    Rome.

Lo! in yon brilliant window-
    niche
  How statue-like I see thee
    stand,
The agate lamp within thy
    hand!
  Ah, Psyche, from the regions
    which
  Are Holy Land!

JAMES RUSSELL LOWELL (1819–1891)

True Love

True love is but an humble, low-born thing,
And hath its food served up in earthen ware;
It is a thing to walk with hand in hand
Through the every-dayness of this work-day world,

Baring its tender feet to every flint,
Yet letting not one heart-beat go astray;
A simple, fire-side thing, whose quiet smile
Can warm earth's poorest hovel to a home.

Such is true love, which steals into the heart
With feet as silent as the lightsome dawn,
That kisses smooth the rough brows of the dark,
And hath its will through blissful gentleness:

A love that gives and takes, that seeth faults,
Not with flaw-seeing eyes like needle points,
But loving-kindly ever looks them down,
With the o'ercoming faith that still forgives;

A love that shall be new and fresh each hour,
As is the sunset's golden mystery,
Or the sweet coming of the evening star.

America

I.

Where the wings of a sunny Dome expand
I saw a Banner in gladsome air—
Starry, like Bernice's Hair—
Afloat in broadened bravery there;
With undulating long-drawn flow,
As rolled Brazilian billows go
Voluminously o'er the Line.
The Land reposed in peace below;
  The children in their glee
Were folded to the exulting heart
  Of young Maternity.

II.

Later, and it streamed in fight
  When tempest mingled with the fray,
And over the spear-point of the shaft
  I saw the ambiguous lightning play.
Valor with Valor strove, and died:
Fierce was Despair, and cruel was Pride;
And the lorn Mother speechless stood,
Pale at the fury of her brood.

III.

Yet later, and the silk did wind
    Her fair cold form;
Little availed the shining shroud,
  Though ruddy in hue, to cheer or warm.
A watcher looked upon her low, and said—
She sleeps, but sleeps, she is not dead.
  But in that sleep contortion showed
The terror of the vision there—
  A silent vision unavowed,
  Revealing earth's foundation bare,
    And Gorgon in her hidden place.

It was a thing of fear to see
So foul a dream upon so fair a face,
And the dreamer lying in that starry shroud.

IV.
But from the trance she sudden broke—
The trance, or death into promoted life;
At her feet a shivered yoke,
And in her aspect turned to heaven
No trace of passion or of strife—
A clear calm look. It spake of pain,
But such as purifies from stain—
Sharp pangs that never come again—
And triumph repressed by knowledge meet,
Power delicate, and hope grown wise,
And youth matured for age's seat—
Law on her brow and empire in her eyes.
So she, with graver air and lifted flag;
While the shadow, chased by light,
Fled along the far-drawn height,
And left her on the crag.

WALT WHITMAN (1819–1892)

A Glimpse

A glimpse through an interstice caught,
Of a crowd of workmen and drivers in a bar-room
    around the stove late of a winter night, and I
    unremark'd seated in a corner,
Of a youth who loves me and whom I love, silently
    approaching and seating himself near, that he
    may hold me by the hand,
A long while amid the noises of coming and going, of
    drinking and oath and smutty jest,
There we two, content, happy in being together,
    speaking little, perhaps not a word.

To a Stranger

Passing stranger! you do not know how longingly I look
    upon you,
You must be he I was seeking, or she I was seeking, (it comes
    to me as of a dream,)
I have somewhere surely lived a life of joy with you,
All is recall'd as we flit by each other, fluid, affectionate,
    chaste, matured,
You grew up with me, were a boy with me or a girl with me,
I ate with you and slept with you, your body has become not
    yours only nor left my body mine only,
You give me the pleasure of your eyes, face, flesh, as we pass,
    you take of my beard, breast, hands, in return,
I am not to speak to you, I am to think of you when I sit alone
    or wake at night alone,
I am to wait, I do not doubt I am to meet you again,
I am to see to it that I do not lose you.

from *I Sing the Body Electric*

This is the female form,
A divine nimbus exhales from it from head to foot,
It attracts with fierce undeniable attraction,
I am drawn by its breath as if I were no more than a
    helpless vapour, all falls aside but myself and it,
Books, art, religion, time, and the visible and solid earth,
    and what was expected of heaven or feared of hell,
    are now consumed,
Mad filaments, ungovernable shoots play out of it, the
    response likewise ungovernable,
Ebb stung by the flow and flow stung by the ebb, love-
    flesh swelling and deliciously aching,
Limitless limpid jets of love hot and enormous,
    quivering jelly of love, white-blow and delirious
    juice,
Bridegroom might of love working surely and softly
    into the prostrate dawn,
Undulating into the willing and yielding day,
Lost in the cleave of the clasping and sweet-fleshed
    day.

This the nucleus—after the child is born of woman,
    man is born of woman,
This the bath of birth, this the merge of small and
    large, and the outlet again.
Be not ashamed women, your privilege encloses the
    rest, and is the exit of the rest,
You are the gates of the body, and you are the gates of
    the soul.

The female contains all qualities and tempers then,
She is in her place and moves with perfect balance,
She is all things duly veiled, she is both passive and
    active,
She is to conceive daughters as well as sons, and sons
    as well as daughters.

As I see my soul reflected in Nature,
As I see through a mist, One with inexpressible
    completeness, sanity, beauty,
See the bent head and arms folded over the breast, the
    Female I see.

EMILY DICKINSON (1830–1886)

Parting

My life closed twice before its close;
It yet remains to see
If Immortality unveil
A third event to me,

So huge, so hopeless to conceive,
As these that twice befell.
Parting is all we know of heaven,
And all we need of hell.

Longing

I envy seas whereon he rides,
  I envy spokes of wheels
Of chariots that him convey,
  I envy speechless hills

That gaze upon his journey;
  How easy all can see
What is forbidden utterly
  As heaven, unto me!

I envy nests of sparrows
  That dot his distant eaves,
The wealthy fly upon his pane,
  The happy, happy leaves

That just abroad his window
  Have summer's leave to be,
The earrings of Pizarro
  Could not obtain for me.

I envy light that wakes him,
  And bells that boldly ring
To tell him it is noon abroad—
  Myself his noon could bring,

Yet interdict my blossom
  And abrogate my bee,
Lest noon in everlasting night
  Drop Gabriel and me.

Heart, We Will Forget Him!

Heart, we will forget him!
  You and I, to-night!
You may forget the warmth he gave,
  I will forget the light.

When you have done, pray tell me,
  That I my thoughts may dim;
Haste! lest while you're lagging,
  I may remember him!

The Brook of the Heart

Have you got a brook in your little heart,
Where bashful flowers blow,
And blushing birds go down to drink,
And shadows tremble so?

And nobody knows, so still it flows,
That any brook is there;
And yet your little draught of life
Is daily drunken there.

Then look out for the little brook in March,
When the rivers overflow,
And the snows come hurrying from the hills,
And the bridges often go.

And later, in August it may be,
When the meadows parching lie,
Beware, lest this little brook of life
Some burning noon go dry!

With a Flower

I hide myself within a flower
That wearing on your breast,
You, unsuspecting, wear me too—
And angels know the rest.

I hide myself within my flower,
That, fading from your vase,
You, unsuspecting, feel for me
Almost a loneliness.

The Little Toil of Love

I had no time to hate, because
The grave would hinder me,
And life was not so ample I
Could finish enmity.

Nor had I time to love; but since
Some industry must be,
The little toil of love, I thought,
Was large enough for me.

Thomas Bailey Aldrich (1836–1907)

Love's Calendar

The Summer comes and the Summer goes;

Wild-
flowers
are fringing
the dusty lanes,
The swallows go darting
through fragrant rains,
Then, all of a sudden—it snows.

Dear Heart, our lives so happily flow,
So lightly we heed the flying hours,
We only know Winter is gone—by the flowers,
We only know Winter is come—by the snow.

Lucinda Matlock

I went to the dances at Chandlerville,
And played snapout at Winchester.
One time we changed partners,
Driving home in the moonlight of middle June,
And then I found Davis.
We were married and lived together for seventy years,
Enjoying, working, raising the twelve children,
Eight of whom we lost
Ere I had reached the age of sixty.
I spun, I wove, I kept the house, I nursed the sick,
I made the garden, and for holiday
Rambled over the fields where sang the larks,
And by Spoon River gathering many a shell,
And many a flower and medicinal weed—
Shouting to the wooded hills, singing to the green valleys.
At ninety-six I had lived enough, that is all,
And passed to a sweet repose.
What is this I hear of sorrow and weariness,
Anger, discontent, and drooping hopes?
Degenerate sons and daughters,
Life is too strong for you—
It takes life to love Life.

JAMES WELDON JOHNSON (1871–1938)

Beauty That is Never Old

When buffeted and beaten by life's storms,
When by the bitter cares of life oppressed,
I want no surer haven than your arms,
I want no sweeter heaven than your breast.

When over my life's way there falls the blight
Of sunless days, and nights of starless skies;
Enough for me, the calm and steadfast light
That softly shines within your loving eyes.

The world, for me, and all the world can hold
Is circled by your arms; for me there lies,
Within the lights and shadows of your eyes,
The only beauty that is never old.

But I Have Not Love

Linnet's eggs in the gorse bushes
So prickly and yellow
Smelling so sweet
In the April sunshine.
              But
                    I have not love.

Eggs in the chaffinches' nest
At the end of the garden hedge
Tiny blue eggs of the hedge sparrow
Hidden below new leaves.
              But
                    I have not love.

The happy tints of summer's curtains
Put up unexpectedly in the night
Upon the young trees
After the dreary winter rains,—
              But
                    I have not love.

The sight of the first celandine.
Of forsythia.
The sight of hayfields by the river
Starred with spring flowers
As I wander through them.
              But
                    I have not love.

The radiance of the children's faces,
Of children's voices
Of children's dancing feet
Under the elms.
The delicate veils of blossoms
Cast as a gossamer mist
Over tree and bush.
                    But
                        I have not love.

All the scents and sounds of the garden,
Of spring.
Of the new year
Coming in at the window
Where I dream.
                    But,—oh—
                        I have not love.

Love [I]

I stood in the rain
Outside that secret window
Where I knew she kept her tryst,
The window I was not supposed to know.
I knew she was there—
I saw her come to the front once,
A paper in her hand,
And sit and read.
Our child was with her, too—
Our child!
She told me they were going to Westchester.

And then I went back to our home to wait,
To tell her of her shame,
My hate,
To drive her out,
To mourn,
To curse,
To say that I had seen,
To say that she had lied.

Yet when she came,
Cold, brave and desirable,
How well I know,
That if I spoke
Or raged
She would then leave
Would never more return—
And so
I
Who desired to scorn
To strike
To slay—

I gulped my rage,
The hate that in me stormed,
The misery—
And smiled,
So covering my madness with a smile.
"Bessie," I said,
"And was your visit pleasant?"
Yet all the while I was a-cold with rage.
I hated,
Groaned.
That night, alone, I strode the streets
And sobbed,
And once (believe it) vomited,
So sore was I at heart.
My business needing me,
I still walked on
That day
And others,
Walking, walking long
And never knowing peace.
And yet,
In time,
She left me anyhow,
My arts to no avail.
But still the pain is here,
Is still in my heart,
My groin,
And it is twenty years.

The Pilgrim

The love I bear you—
Is destroying,—
A canker
That eats at my heart.

And yet
It is
The most perfect thing
That I possess,—
A treasure
The value of which
Is beyond measuring.

There is
Within your spirit,—
The little flame that is you,—
The light
That lights for me
This otherwise dark way
Along which I fumble
And fail.
When all is well between us
All is well, indeed.
But when you are unhappy,
Or I
Because of you,
But most so when 'tis I
Who make you so
'Tis then the spirit sinks
To a dark and rainy land
Where only misery
And unrest
Abide.

Oh, you may never know.
For then my heart mourns deeply.
And forth from it
There goes
Into the shadow
That is not life
But time,
Into the silence
That is space,
Its shadow,
Its wraith,
The ghost of its own sorrow
That must pilgrimage
To where'er you are,
Your heart,
Its grail.
And it must find you, too,
Where'er you are
And whimper at your door
That you may open to it
And understand.

Oh,
Have you not heard?
Do you not know?
Do you not feel?
That without,
Ragged,
Footsore,
Hungry
Is love,—
This wraith of my misery,—
That waits
And calls
And would be
Let in
To you.

Love Plaint

I have sought to fetter love,—
To bind it.
But love is like the wind
Stirring in the tall grass at night
Under great trees
In the dark.
It may not be seen
Or fettered
But only felt.
Or,
Again,
Love is like a distant voice
On sea or land,
In fog or storm
That calls and calls
And speaks of need.
A sweet voice that would give.
Or love is like a perfume
That the wind brings
But that one cannot place
Or know,—
A rumor of old things that were
Or yet may be
Or are,
But that one may not hold.
It dwells where shadow is
And song
And dream,
And sings
Or weeps
Or calls
And, oh, the ache
Of that elusive call.

But I,—
I sought to bind love
And it fled.
And now the searing day has come,—
The blare and crash of life,—
The long hot day of want—
And now the grit and dust
Of life's hard, thundering wheels
Are on my lips
And in my eyes
Inflamed and yet made tender
By Love's lips.

PAUL LAURENCE DUNBAR (1872–1906)

A Negro Love Song

Seen my lady home las' night,
  Jump back honey, jump back.
Hel' huh han' an' sque'z it tight,
  Jump back honey, jump back.
Heahd huh sigh a little sigh,
Seen a light gleam f'um huh eye,
An' a smile go flitin' by—
  Jump back honey, jump back.

Heahd de win' blow thoo de pines,
  Jump back honey, jump back.
Mockin' bird was singin, fine,
  Jump back honey, jump back.
An' my hea't was beatin' so,
When I reached my lady's do',
Dat I couldn't ba' to go—
  Jump back, honey, jump back.

Put my ahm aroun' huh wais',
  Jump back, honey, jump back.
Raised huh lips an took a tase',
  Jump back, honey, jump back.
Love me honey, love me true?
Love me well ez I love you?
An' she ansawhd: "'Cose I do"—
  Jump back, honey, jump back.

AMY LOWELL (1874–1925)

The Captured Goddess

Over the housetops,
Above the rotating chimney-pots,
I have seen a shiver of amethyst,
And blue and cinnamon have flickered
A moment,
At the far end of a dusty street.

Through sheeted rain
Has come a lustre of crimson,
And I have watched moonbeams
Hushed by a film of palest green.

It was her wings,
Goddess!
Who stepped over the clouds,
And laid her rainbow feathers
Aslant on the currents of the air.
I followed her for long,
With gazing eyes and stumbling feet.
I cared not where she led me,
My eyes were full of colors:
Saffrons, rubies, the yellows of beryls,
And the indigo-blue of quartz;
Flights of rose, layers of chrysoprase,
Points of orange, spirals of vermilion,
The spotted gold of tiger-lily petals,
The loud pink of bursting hydrangeas.
I followed,
And watched for the flashing of her wings.

In the city I found her,
The narrow-streeted city.
In the market-place I came upon her,
Bound and trembling.
Her fluted wings were fastened to her sides with cords,
She was naked and cold,
For that day the wind blew
Without sunshine.

Men chaffered for her,
They bargained in silver and gold,
In copper, in wheat,
And called their bids across the market-place.

The Goddess wept.

Hiding my face I fled,
And the grey wind hissed behind me,
Along the narrow streets.

Robert Frost (1874–1963)

Two Look at Two

Love and forgetting might have carried them
A little further up the mountain side
With night so near, but not much further up.
They must have halted soon in any case
With thoughts of the path back, how rough it was
With rock and washout, and unsafe in darkness;
When they were halted by a tumbled wall
With barbed-wire binding. They stood facing this,
Spending what onward impulse they still had
In one last look the way they must not go,
On up the failing path, where, if a stone
Or earthslide moved at night, it moved itself;
No footstep moved it. "This is all," they sighed,
"Good-night to woods." But not so; there was more.
A doe from round a spruce stood looking at them
Across the wall, as near the wall as they.
She saw them in their field, they her in hers.
The difficulty of seeing what stood still,
Like some up-ended boulder split in two,
Was in her clouded eyes: they saw no fear there.
She seemed to think that two thus they were safe.
Then, as if they were something that, though strange,
She could not trouble her mind with too long,
She sighed and passed unscared along the wall.
"*This*, then, is all. What more is there to ask?"
But no, not yet. A snort to bid them wait.
A buck from round the spruce stood looking at them
Across the wall as near the wall as they.
Not the same doe come back into her place.
He viewed them quizzically with jerks of head,
As if to ask, "Why don't you make some motion?
Or give some sign of life? Because you can't.
I doubt if you're as living as you look."
Thus till he had them almost feeling dared

To stretch a proffering hand—and a spell-breaking.
Then he too passed unscared along the wall.
Two had seen two, whichever side you spoke from.
"This *must* be all." It was all. Still they stood,
A great wave from it going over them,
As if the earth in one unlooked-for favor
Had made them certain earth returned their love.

Love and a Question

A Stranger came to the door at eve,
  And he spoke the bridegroom fair.
He bore a green-white stick in his hand,
  And, for all burden, care.
He asked with the eyes more than the lips
  For a shelter for the night,
And he turned and looked at the road afar
  Without a window light.

The bridegroom came forth into the porch
  With 'Let us look at the sky,
And question what of the night to be,
  Stranger, you and I.'
The woodbine leaves littered the yard,
  The woodbine berries were blue,
Autumn, yes, winter was in the wind;
  'Stranger, I wish I knew.'

Within, the bride in the dusk alone
  Bent over the open fire,
Her face rose-red with the glowing coal
  And the thought of the heart's desire.
The bridegroom looked at the weary road,
  Yet saw but her within,
And wished her heart in a case of gold
  And pinned with a silver pin.

The bridegroom thought it little to give
  A dole of bread, a purse,
A heartfelt prayer for the poor of God,
  Or for the rich a curse;
But whether or not a man was asked
  To mar the love of two
By harboring woe in the bridal house,
  The bridegroom wished he knew.

The Investment

Over back where they
speak of life as
staying
("You couldn't call it
living, for it
ain't"),
There was an old,
old house
renewed with
paint,
And in it a piano
loudly playing.

Out in the ploughed
ground in the
cold a digger,
Among unearthed potatoes standing still,
Was counting winter dinners, one a hill,
With half an ear to the piano's vigor.

All that piano and new paint back there,
Was it some money suddenly come into?
Or some extravagance young love had been to?
Or old love on an impulse not to care—

Not to sink under being man and wife
But get some color and music out of life?

ROBERT FROST

Wind and Window Flower

Lovers, forget your love,
  And list to the love of these.
She a window flower,
  And he a winter breeze.

When the frosty window veil
  Was melted down at noon,
And the cagèd yellow bird
  Hung over her in tune,

He marked her through the pane
  He could not help but mark,
And only passed her by,
  To come again at dark.

He was a winter wind,
  Concerned with ice and snow,
Dead weeds and unmated birds,
  And little of love could know.

But he sighed upon the sill,
  He gave the sash a shake,
As witness all within
  Who lay that night awake.

Perchance he half prevailed
  To win her for the flight
From the firelit looking-glass
  And warm stove-window light.

But the flower leaned aside
  And thought of naught to say,
And morning found the breeze
  A hundred miles away.

Explanations of Love

There is a place where love begins and a place where love ends.
There is a touch of two hands that foils all dictionaries.
There is a look of eyes fierce as a big Bethlehem open-house furnace or a little green-eyed acetylene torch.
There are single careless bywords portentous as the big bend in the Mississippi River.
Hands, eyes, bywords—out of these love makes battle-grounds and workshops.
There is a pair of shoes love wears and the coming is a mystery.
There is a warning love sends and the cost of it is never written till long afterward.
There are explanations of love in all languages and not one found wiser than this:
There is a place where love begins and a place where love ends—and love asks nothing.

WALLACE STEVENS (1879–1955)

Restatement of Romance

The night knows nothing of the chants of night.
It is what it is as I am what I am:
And in perceiving this I best perceive myself

And you. Only we two may interchange
Each in the other what each has to give.
Only we two are one, not you and night.

Nor night and I, but you and I, alone,
So much alone, so deeply by ourselves,
So far beyond the casual solitudes,

That night is only the background of our selves,
Supremely true each to its separate self,
In the pale light that each upon the other throws.

WILLIAM CARLOS WILLIAMS (1883–1963)

To Mark Anthony in Heaven

This quiet morning light
reflected, how many times
from grass and trees and clouds
enters my north room
touching the walls with
grass and clouds and trees.
Anthony,
trees and grass and clouds.
Why did you follow
that beloved body
with your ships at Actium?
I hope it was because
you knew her inch by inch
from slanting feet upward
to the roots of her hair
and down again and that
you saw her
above the battle's fury—
clouds and trees and grass—

For then you are
listening in heaven.

Portrait of a Lady

Your thighs are appletrees
whose blossoms touch the sky.
Which sky? The sky
where Watteau hung a lady's
slipper. Your knees
are a southern breeze—or
a gust of snow. Agh! what
sort of man was Fragonard?
—as if that answered
anything. Ah, yes—below
the knees, since the tune
drops that way, it is
one of those white summer days,
the tall grass of your ankles
flickers upon the shore—
Which shore?—
the sand clings to my lips—
Which shore?
Agh, petals maybe. How
should I know?
Which shore? Which shore?
I said petals from an appletree.

After Parting

Oh I have sown my love so wide
That he will find it everywhere;
It will awake him in the night,
It will enfold him in the air.

I set my shadow in his sight
And I have winged it with desire,
That it may be a cloud by day
And in the night a shaft of fire.

The Look

Strephon kissed me in the spring,
  Robin in the fall,
But Colin only looked at me
  And never kissed at all.

Strephon's kiss was lost in jest,
  Robin's lost in play,
But the kiss in Colin's eyes
  Haunts me night and day.

The Years

To-night I close my eyes and see
A strange procession passing me—
The years before I saw your face
Go by me with a wistful grace;
They pass, the sensitive shy years,
As one who strives to dance, half blind with tears.

The years went by and never knew
That each one brought me nearer you;
Their path was narrow and apart
And yet it led me to your heart—
Oh sensitive shy years, oh lonely years,
That strove to sing with voices drowned in tears.

The Kiss

Before you kissed me only winds of heaven
Had kissed me, and the tenderness of rain—
Now you have come, how can I care for kisses
Like theirs again?

I sought the sea, she sent her winds to meet me,
They surged about me singing of the south—
I turned my head away to keep still holy
Your kiss upon my mouth.

And swift sweet rains of shining April weather
Found not my lips where living kisses are;
I bowed my head lest they put out my glory
As rain puts out a star.

I am my love's and he is mine forever,
Sealed with a seal and safe forevermore—
Think you that I could let a beggar enter
Where a king stood before?

SARA TEASDALE

Spring Night

The park is filled with night and fog,
  The veils are drawn about the world,
The drowsy lights along the paths
  Are dim and pearled.

Gold and gleaming the empty streets,
  Gold and gleaming the misty lake,
The mirrored lights like sunken swords,
  Glimmer and shake.

Oh, is it not enough to be
Here with this beauty over me?

My throat should ache with praise, and I
Should kneel in joy beneath the sky.
O beauty, are you not enough?
Why am I crying after love
With youth, a singing voice, and eyes
To take earth's wonder with surprise?

Why have I put off my pride,
Why am I unsatisfied,—
I, for whom the pensive night
Binds her cloudy hair with light,—
I, for whom all beauty burns
Like incense in a million urns?
O beauty, are you not enough?
Why am I crying after love?

ELINOR WYLIE (1885–1928)

A Puritan's Ballad

My love came up from Barnegat,
   The sea was in his eyes;
He trod as softly as a cat
   And told me terrible lies.

His hair was yellow as new-cut pine
   In shavings curled and feathered;
I thought how silver it would shine
   By cruel winters weathered.

But he was in his twentieth year,
   This time I'm speaking of;
We were head over heels in love with fear
   And half a-feared of love.

His feet were used to treading a gale
   And balancing thereon;
His face was brown as a foreign sail
   Threadbare against the sun.

His arms were thick as hickory logs
  Whittled to little wrists;
Strong as the teeth of terrier dogs
  Were the fingers of his fists.

Within his arms I feared to sink
  Where lions shook their manes,
And dragons drawn in azure ink
  Leapt quickened by his veins.

Dreadful his strength and length of limb
  As the sea to foundering ships;
I dipped my hands in love for him
  No deeper than their tips.

But our palms were welded by a flame
  The moment we came to part,
And on his knuckles I read my name
  Enscrolled within a heart

And something made our wills to bend
  As wild as trees blown over;
We were no longer friend and friend,
  But only lover and lover.

"In seven weeks or seventy years—
  God grant it may be sooner!—
I'll make the handkerchief for your tears
  From the sails of my captain's schooner.

"We'll wear our loves like wedding rings
  Long polished to our touch;
We shall be busy with other things
  And they cannot bother us much.

"When you are skimming the wrinkled cream
  And your ring clinks on the pan,
You'll say to yourself in a pensive dream,
  'How wonderful a man!'

"When I am slitting a fish's head
    And my ring clanks on the knife,
I'll say with thanks, as a prayer is said,
    'How beautiful a wife!'

"And I shall fold my decorous paws
    In velvet smooth and deep
Like a kitten that covers up its claws
    To sleep and sleep and sleep.

"Like a little blue pigeon you shall bow
    Your bright alarming crest;
In the crook of my arm you'll lay your brow
    To rest and rest and rest."

Will he never come back from Barnegat
    With thunder in his eyes,
Treading as soft as a tiger cat
    To tell me terrible lies?

EZRA POUND (1885–1972)

An Immorality

Sing we for love and idleness,
Naught else is worth the having.

Though I have been in many a land,
There is naught else in living.

And I would rather have my sweet,
Though rose-leaves die of grieving,

Than do high deeds in Hungary
To pass all men's believing.

EZRA POUND

The River-Merchant's Wife: A Letter

While my hair was still cut straight across my forehead
I played about the front gate, pulling flowers.
You came by on bamboo stilts,
     playing horse.
You walked about my seat,
     playing with blue plums.
And we went on living in the
     village of Chokan:
Two small people, without
     dislike or suspicion.

At fourteen I married My Lord you.
I never laughed, being bashful.
Lowering my head, I looked at the wall.
Called to, a thousand times, I never looked back.

At fifteen I stopped scowling,
I desired my dust to be mingled with yours
Forever and forever and forever.
Why should I climb the look out?

At sixteen you departed,
You went into far Ku-to-yen, by the river of swirling eddies,
And you have been gone five months.
The monkeys make a sorrowful noise overhead.
You dragged your feet when you went out.
By the gate now, the moss is grown, the different mosses,
Too deep to clear them away!
The leaves fall early this autumn, in wind.
 The paired butterflies are already yellow with August
Over the grass in the West garden;
They hurt me. I grow older.
If you are coming down through the narrows of the
     river Kiang,
Please let me know beforehand,
And I will come to meet you
     As far as Cho-fu-sa.

HILDA DOOLITTLE (1886–1961)

Eros

I

Where is he taking us
now that he has turned back?

Where will this take us,
this fever,
spreading into light?

Nothing we have ever felt,
nothing we have dreamt,
or conjured in the night
or fashioned in loneliness,
can equal this.

Where is he taking us,
Eros,
now that he has turned back?

II

My mouth is wet with your life,
my eyes blinded with your face,
a heart itself which feels
the intimate music.

My mind is caught,
dimmed with it,
(where is love taking us?)
my lips are wet with your life.

In my body were pearls cast,
shot with Ionian tints, purple,
vivid through the white.

III

Keep love and he wings
with his bow,
up, mocking us,
keep love and he taunts us
and escapes.

Keep love and he sways apart
in another world,
outdistancing us.

Keep love and he mocks,
ah, bitter and sweet,
your sweetness is more cruel
than your hurt.

Honey and salt,
fire burst from the rocks
to meet fire
spilt from Hesperus.

Fire darted aloft and met fire,
and in that moment
love entered us.

IV

Could Eros be kept,
he was prisoned long since
and sick with imprisonment,
could Eros be kept,
others would have taken him
and crushed out his life.

Could Eros be kept,
we had sinned against the great god,
we too might have prisoned him outright.

Could Eros be kept,
nay, thank him and the bright goddess
that he left us.

V

Ah love is bitter and sweet,
but which is more sweet
the bitterness or the sweetness,
none has spoken it.

Love is bitter,
but can salt taint sea-flowers,
grief, happiness?

Is it bitter to give back
love to your lover if he crave it?

Is it bitter to give back
love to your lover if he wish it
for a new favourite,
who can say,
or is it sweet?

Is it sweet to possess utterly,
or is it bitter,
bitter as ash?

VI

I had thought myself frail,
a petal
with light equal
on leaf and under-leaf.

I had thought myself frail;
a lamp,
shell, ivory or crust of pearl,
about to fall shattered,
with flame spent.

I cried:

"I must perish,
I am deserted in this darkness,
an outcast, desperate,"
such fire rent me with Hesperus,

Then the day broke.

What need of a lamp
when day lightens us,
what need to bind love
when love stands
with such radiant wings over us?

What need—
yet to sing love,
love must first shatter us.

CONRAD AIKEN (1889–1973)

Music I Heard

Music I heard with you was more than music,
And bread I broke with you was more than bread;
Now that I am without you, all is desolate;
All that was once so beautiful is dead.

Your hands once touched this table and this silver,
And I have seen your fingers hold this glass.
These things do not remember you, beloved,
And yet your touch upon them will not pass.

For it was in my heart you moved among them,
And blessed them with your hands and with your eyes;
And in my heart they will remember always,—
They knew you once, O beautiful and wise.

 CONRAD AIKEN

The Quarrel

Suddenly, after the quarrel, while we waited,
Disheartened, silent, with downcast looks,
    nor stirred
Eyelid nor finger, hopeless both, yet hoping
    Against all hope to unsay the sundering word:

While all the room's stillness deepened, deepened
    about us,
    And each of us crept his thought's way
      to discover
    How, with as little sound as the fall of a leaf,
    The shadow had fallen, and lover quarreled
      with lover;

    And while, in the quiet, I marveled—alas, alas—
    At your deep beauty, your tragic beauty, torn
    As the pale flower is torn by the wanton sparrow—
This beauty, pitied and loved, and now forsworn;

It was then, when the instant darkened to its
    darkest,—
When faith was lost with hope, and the rain
    conspired
To strike its gray arpeggios against our heartstrings,—
When love no longer dared, and scarcely
    desired:

It was then that suddenly, in the neighbor's room,
The music started: that brave quartette of strings
Breaking out of the stillness, as out of
    our stillness,
Like the indomitable heart of life
    that sings

When all is lost; and startled from our sorrow,
 Tranced from our grief by that diviner grief,
 We raised remembering eyes, each looked at other,
 Blinded with tears of joy; and another leaf

Fell silently as that first; and in the instant
The shadow had gone, our quarrel became absurd;
And we rose, to the angelic voices of the music,
And I touched your hand, and we kissed, without a word.

ROBINSON JEFFERS (1887–1962)

Divinely Superfluous Beauty

The storm-dances of gulls, the barking game of seals,
Over and under the ocean . . .
Divinely superfluous beauty
Rules the games, presides over destinies, makes trees grow
And hills tower, waves fall.
The incredible beauty of joy
Stars with fire the joining of lips, O let our loves too
Be joined, there is not a maiden
Burns and thirsts for love
More than my blood for you, by the shore of seals while
    the wings
Weave like a web in the air
Divinely superfluous beauty.

The Maid's Thought

Why listen, even the water is sobbing for something.
The west wind is dead, the waves
Forget to hate the cliff, in the upland canyons
Whole hillsides burst aglow
With golden broom. Dear how it rained last month,
And every pool was rimmed
With sulphury pollen dust of the wakening pines.
Now tall and slender suddenly
The stalks of purple iris blaze by the brooks,
The penciled ones on the hill:
This deerweed shivers with gold, the white globe-tulips
Blow out their silky bubbles,
But in the next glen bronze-bells nod, the does
Scalded by some hot longing
Can hardly set their pointed hoofs to expect
Love but they crush a flower;
Shells pair on the rock, birds mate, the moths fly double.
O it is time for us now
Mouth kindling mouth to entangle our maiden bodies
To make that burning flower.

For Una

1

I built her a tower when I was young—
Sometime she will die—
I built it with my hands, I hung
Stones in the sky.

Old but still strong I climb the stone—
Sometime she will die—
Climb the steep rough steps alone,
And weep in the sky.

Never weep, never weep.

2

Never be astonished, dear.
Expect change.
Nothing is strange.

We have seen the human race
Capture all its dreams,
All expect peace.

We have watched mankind like Christ
Toil up and up,
To be hanged at the top.

No longer envying the birds,
That ancient prayer for
Wings granted: therefore

The heavy sky over London,
Stallion-hoofed,
Falls on the roofs.

These are the falling years,
They will go deep,
Never weep, never weep.

With clear eyes explore the pit.
Watch the great fall
With religious awe.

3

It is not Europe alone that is falling
Into blood and fire.
Decline and fall have been dancing in all men's souls
For a long while.

Sometime at the last gasp comes peace
To every soul.
Never to mine until I find out and speak
The things that I know.

4

Tomorrow I will take up that heavy poem again
About Ferguson, deceived and jealous man
Who bawled for the truth, the truth, and failed to endure
Its first least gleam. That poem bores me, and I hope will bore
Any sweet soul that reads it, being some ways
My very self but mostly my antipodes;
But having waved the heavy artillery to fire
I must hammer on to an end.

                    Tonight, dear,
Let's forget all that, that and the war,
And enisle ourselves a little beyond time,
You with this Irish whiskey, I with red wine,
While the stars go over the sleepless ocean,
And sometime after midnight I'll pluck you a wreath
Of chosen ones; we'll talk about love and death,
Rock-solid themes, old and deep as the sea,
Admit nothing more timely, nothing less real
While the stars go over the timeless ocean,
And when they vanish we'll have spent the night well.

JOHN CROWE RANSOM (1888–1974)

Blue Girls

Twirling your blue skirts, travelling the sward
Under the towers of your seminary,
Go listen to your teachers old and contrary
Without believing a word.

Tie the white fillets then about your hair
And think no more of what will come to pass
Than bluebirds that go walking on the grass
And chattering on the air.

Practice your beauty, blue girls, before it fail;
And I will cry with my loud lips and publish
Beauty which all our power shall never establish,
It is so frail.

For I could tell you a story which is true;
I know a lady with a terrible tongue,
Blear eyes fallen from blue,
All her perfections tarnished—yet it is not long
Since she was lovelier than any of you.

JOHN CROWE RANSOM

Parting Without A Sequel

She has finished and sealed the letter
At last, which he so richly deserved,
With characters venomous and
hatefully curved,
And nothing could be better.

But even as she gave it,
Saying to the blue-capped
functioner of doom,
'Into his hands,' she hoped the leering groom
Might somewhere lose and leave it.

Then all the blood
Forsook the face. She was too pale for tears,
Observing the ruin of her younger years.
She went and stood

Under her father's vaunting oak
Who kept his peace in wind and sun, and glistened
Stoical in the rain; to whom she listened
If he spoke.

And now the agitation of the rain
Rasped his sere leaves, and he talked low and gentle,
Reproaching the wan daughter by the lintel;
Ceasing, and beginning again.

Away went the messenger's
bicycle,
His serpent's track went up
the hill forever,
And all the time she stood
there hot as fever
And cold as any icicle.

EDNA ST. VINCENT MILLAY (1892–1950)

Ashes of Life

Love has gone, and left me and the days are all alike.
　Eat I must, and sleep I will—and would that night were here!
But ah, to lie awake and hear the slow hours strike!
　Would that it were day again, with twilight near!

Love has gone and left me, and I don't know what to do;
　This or that or what you will is all the same to me;
But all the things that I begin I leave before I'm through—
　There's little use in anything as far as I can see.

Love has gone and left me, and the neighbors knock and
　　borrow,
　And life goes on forever like the gnawing of a mouse.
And tomorrow and tomorrow and tomorrow and to-
　　morrow
　There's this little street and this little house.

The Dream

Love, if I weep it will not matter,
  And if you laugh I shall not care;
Foolish am I to think about it,
  But it is good to feel you there.

Love, in my sleep I dreamed of waking,—
  White and awful the moonlight reached
Over the floor, and somewhere, somewhere
  There was a shutter loose,—it screeched!—

Swung in the wind!—and no wind blowing!—
  I was afraid, and turned to you,
Put out my hand to you for comfort,—
  And you were gone! Cold, cold as dew,

Under my hand the moonlight lay!
  Love, if you laugh I shall not care,
But if I weep it will not matter,—
  Ah, it is good to feel you there!

Ebb

I know what my heart is like
　　Since your love died:
It is like a hollow ledge
Holding a little pool
　　Left there by the tide,
　　　A little tepid pool,
Drying inward from the edge.

Armenonville

By the lake at Armenonville in the Bois de Boulogne
Small begonias had been set in the embankment, both pink
    and red;
With polished leaf and brittle, juicy stem;
They covered the embankment; there were wagon-loads
    of them,
Charming and neat, gay colours in the warm shade.

We had preferred a table near the lake, half out of view,
Well out of hearing, for a voice not raised above
A low, impassioned question and its low reply.
We both leaned forward with our elbows on the table, and you
Watched my mouth while I answered, and it made me shy.
I looked about, but the waiters knew we were in love,
And matter-of-factly left us blissfully alone.

There swam across the lake, as I looked aside, avoiding
Your eyes for a moment, there swam from under the pink and
    red begonias
A small creature; I thought it was a water-rat; it swam very well,
In complete silence, and making no ripples at all
Hardly; and when suddenly I turned again to you,
Aware that you were speaking, and perhaps had been speaking
    for some time,
I was aghast at my absence, for truly I did not know
Whether you had been asking or telling.

Recuerdo

We were very tired, we were very merry—
We had gone back and forth all night on the ferry.
It was bare and bright, and smelled like a stable—
But we looked into a fire, we leaned across a table,
We lay on a hill-top underneath the moon;
And the whistles kept blowing, and the dawn came soon.

We were very tired, we were very
merry—
We had gone back and forth all
night on the ferry;
And you ate an apple, and I
ate a pear,
From a dozen of each we
had bought somewhere;
And the sky went wan, and the
wind came cold,
And the sun rose dripping, a
bucketful of gold.

We were very tired, we were
very merry—
We had gone back and forth all night on the ferry.
We hailed, "Good-morrow, mother!" to a shawl-covered head,
And bought a morning paper, which neither of us read;
And she wept, "God bless you!" for the apples and pears,
And we gave her all our money but our subway fares.

Archibald MacLeish (1892–1982)

"Not Marble, Nor the Gilded Monuments"

The praisers of women in their proud and beautiful poems
Naming the grave mouth and the hair and the eyes
Boasted those they loved should be forever remembered
These were lies

The words sound but the face in the Istrian sun is forgotten
The poet speaks but to her dead ears no more
The sleek throat is gone—and the breast that was troubled
    to listen
Shadow from door

Therefore I will not praise your knees nor your fine walking
Telling you men shall remember your name as long
As lips move or breath is spent or the iron of English
Rings from a tongue

I shall say you were young and your arms straight and your
    mouth scarlet
I shall say you will die and none will remember you
Your arms change and none remember the swish of your
    garments
Nor the click of your shoe

Not with my hand's strength not with difficult labor
Springing the obstinate words to the bones of your breast
And the stubborn line to your young stride and the breath to
    your breathing
And the beat to your haste
Shall I prevail on the hearts of unborn men to remember

(What is a dead girl but a shadowy ghost
Or a dead man's voice but a distant and vain affirmation
Like dream words most)

Therefore I will not speak of the undying glory of women
I will say you were young and straight and your skin fair
And you stood in the door and the sun was shadow of leaves
    on your shoulders
And a leaf on your hair
I will not speak of the famous beauty of dead women
I will say the shape of a leaf lay once on your hair
Till the world ends and the eyes are out and the mouths
    broken
Look! It is there!

Archibald MacLeish

Poem In Prose

This poem is for my wife
I have made it plainly and honestly
The mark is on it
Like the burl on the knife

I have not made it for praise
She has no more need for praise
Than summer has
On the bright days

In all that becomes a woman
Her words and her ways are beautiful
Love's lovely duty
The well-swept room

Wherever she is there is sun
And time and a sweet air
Peace is there
Work done

There are always curtains and flowers
And candles and baked bread
And a cloth spread
And a clean house

Her voice when she sings is a voice
At dawn by a freshening sea
Where the wave leaps in the
Wind and rejoices

Wherever she is it is now
It is here where the apples are
Here in the stars
In the quick hour

The greatest and richest good—
My own life to live—
This she has given me

If giver could

DOROTHY PARKER (1893–1967)

De Profundis

Oh, is it, then, Utopian
To hope that I may meet a man
Who'll not relate, in accents suave,
The tales of girls he used to have?

General Review of the Sex Situation

Woman wants monogamy;
Man delights in novelty.
Love is woman's moon and sun;
Man has other forms of fun.
Woman lives but in her lord;
Count to ten, and man is bored.
With this the gist and sum of it,
What earthly good can come of it?

E.E. Cummings (1894–1962)

Amores

I

consider O
woman this
my body.
for it has

lain
with empty arms
upon the giddy hills
to dream of you,

approve these
firm unsated
eyes
which have beheld

night's speechless carnival
the painting
of the dark
with meteors

streaming from playful
immortal hands
the bursting
of the wafted stars

(in time to come you shall
remember of this night amazing
ecstasies   slowly,
in the glutted

heart fleet
flowerterrible
memories
shall

rise, slowly
return upon the
                    red elected lips

scaleless visions)

II

there is a
moon sole
in the blue
night

        amorous of waters
tremulous,
blinded with silence the
undulous heaven yearns where

in tense starlessness
anoint with ardor
the yellow lover

stands in the dumb dark
svelte
and
urgent

        (again
love i slowly
gather
of thy languorous mouth the

thrilling
flower)

III

as is the sea marvelous
from god's
hands which sent her forth
to sleep upon the world

and the earth withers
the moon crumbles
one by one
stars flutter into dust

but the sea
does not change
and she goes forth out of hands and
she returns into hands

and is with sleep . . .

love,
            the breaking

of your
            soul
            upon
my lips

IV

if i believe
in death be sure
of this
it is

because you have loved me,
moon and sunset
stars and flowers
gold crescendo and silver muting

of seatides
i trusted not,
                    one night
when in my fingers

drooped your shining body
when my heart
sang between your perfect
breasts

darkness and beauty of stars
was on my mouth petals danced
against my eyes
and down

the singing reaches of
my soul
spoke
the green-

greeting pale-
departing irrevocable
sea
i knew thee death.

        and when
i have offered up each fragrant
night, when all my days
shall have before a certain

face become
white
perfume
only,

      from the ashes
then
thou wilt rise and thou
wilt come to her and brush

the mischief from her eyes and fold
her
mouth the new
flower with

thy unimaginable
wings, where dwells the breath
of all persisting stars

V

the glory is fallen out of
the sky the last immortal
leaf
is

dead and the gold
year
a formal spasm
in the

dust
this is the passing of all shining things
therefore we also
blandly

into receptive
earth, O let
us
descend

take
shimmering wind
these fragile splendors from
us crumple them hide

them in thy breath drive
them in nothingness
for we
would sleep

this is the passing of all shining things
no lingering no backward-
wondering be unto
us O

soul, but straight
glad feet fearruining
and glorygirded
faces

lead us
into the
serious
steep

darkness

VI

i like
to think that on
the flower you gave me when we
loved

     the far-
departed mouth sweetly–saluted
lingers.
      if one marvel

seeing the hunger of my
lips for a dead thing,
i shall instruct
him silently with becoming

steps to seek
your face   and i
entreat, by certain foolish perfect
hours

     dead too,
if that he come receive
him as your lover sumptuously
being

kind
     because i trust him to
your grace, and for
in his own land

he is called death.

VII

O Distinct
Lady of my unkempt adoration
if i have made
a fragile certain

song under the window of your soul
it is not like any songs
(the singers the others
they have been faithful

to many things and which
die
i have been sometimes true
to Nothing and which lives

they were fond of the handsome
moon   never spoke ill of the
pretty stars   and to
the serene the complicated

and the obvious
they were faithful
and which i despise,
frankly

admitting i have been true
only to the noise of worms.
in the eligible day
under the unaccountable sun)

Distinct Lady
swiftly take
my fragile certain song
that we may watch together

how behind the doomed
exact smile for life's
placid obscure palpable
carnival where to a normal

melody of probable violins dance
the square virtues and the oblong sins
perfectly
gesticulate the accurate

strenuous lips of incorruptible
Nothing   under the ample
sun, under the insufficient
day under the noise of worms

VIII

your little voice
                  Over the wires came leaping
and i felt suddenly
dizzy
               With the jostling and shouting of merry flowers
wee skipping high-heeled flames
courtesied before my eyes
                     or twinkling over to my side
Looked up
with impertinently exquisite faces
floating hands were laid upon me
I was whirled and tossed into delicious dancing
up
Up
with the pale important
                   stars and the Humorous
                         moon
dear girl
How i was crazy how i cried when i heard
                    over time
and tide and death
leaping
Sweetly
      your voice

Thy fingers make early flowers of

Thy fingers make early flowers of
all things.
thy hair mostly the hours love:
a smoothness which
sings, saying
(though love be a day)
do not fear, we will go amaying.

Thy whitest feet crisply are straying
Always
thy moist eyes are at kisses playing,
whose strangeness much
says; singing
(though love be a day)
for which girl art thou flowers bringing?

To be thy lips is a sweet thing
and small.
Death, Thee i call rich beyond wishing
if this thou catch,
else missing.
(though love be a day
and life be nothing, it shall not stop kissing).

My Love

My love
thy hair is one kingdom
   the king whereof is darkness
thy forehead is flight of flowers

thy head is a quick forest
   filled with sleeping birds
thy breasts are swarms of white bees
   upon the bough of thy body
thy body to me is April
in whose armpits is the approach of spring

thy thighs are white horses yoked to a chariot of kings
they are the striking of a good minstrel
between them always is a pleasant song

my love
thy head is a casket
   of the cool jewel of thy mind
the hair of thy head is one warrior
   innocent of defeat
the hair upon thy shoulders is an army
   with victory and with trumpets

thy legs are the trees of dreaming
whose fruit is the very eatage of forgetfulness

thy lips are satraps in scarlet
   in whose kiss is the combining of kings
thy wrists
are holy
   which are the keepers of the keys of thy blood
thy feet upon thy ankles are flowers in vases of silver

in thy beauty is the dilemma of flutes

   thy eyes are the betrayal
of bells comprehended through incense

Somewhere I Have Never Travelled, Gladly Beyond

somewhere i have never travelled, gladly beyond
any experience, your eyes have their silence;
in your most frail gesture are things which enclose me,
or which i cannot touch because they are too near

your slightest look easily
    will unclose me
though i have closed
    myself as fingers,
you open always petal by petal
    myself as Spring opens
(touching skilfully, mysteriously) her
    first rose

or if your wish be to close me, i and
my life will shut very beautifully, suddenly,
as when the heart of this flower imagines
the snow carefully everywhere descending;

nothing which we are to perceive in this world equals
the power of your intense fragility: whose texture
compels me with the colour of its countries,
rendering death and forever with each breathing

(i do not know what it is about you that closes
and opens; only something in me understands
the voice of your eyes is deeper than all roses)
nobody, not even the rain, has such small hands

MARK VAN DOREN (1894–1972)

Private Worship

She lay there in the stone folds of his life
Like a blue flower in granite—this he knew;
And knew how now inextricably the petals
Clung to the rock; recessed beyond his hand-thrust;
More deeply in, past more forgotten windings
Than his rude tongue could utter, praising her.

He praised her with his eyes, beholding oddly
Not what another saw, but
        what she added—
Thinning today and
        shattering with a slow
                smile—
To the small flower within, to
        the saved secret.
She was not to have—except
        that something,
Always like petals falling,
        entered him.

She was not his to keep—
        except the brightness,
Flowing from her, that lived in
        him like dew;
And the kind flesh he could
        remember touching,
And the unconscious lips, and
        both her eyes:
These lay in him like leaves—
        beyond the last turn
Breathing the rocky darkness till it bloomed.

It was not large, this chamber of the blue flower,
Nor could the scent escape; nor the least color
Ebb from that place and stain the outer stone.
Nothing upon his grey sides told the fable,
Nothing of love or lightness, nothing of song;
Nothing of her at all. Yet he could fancy—

Oh, he could feel where petals spread their softness,
Gathered from windfalls of her when she smiled;
Growing some days, he thought, as if to burst him—
Oh, he could see the split halves, and the torn flower
Fluttering in sudden sun; and see the great stain—
Oh, he could see what tears had done to stone.

F. Scott Fitzgerald (1896–1940)

My First Love

All my ways she wove of light
  Wove them half alive,
Made them warm and beauty-bright . . .
  So the shining, ambient air
Clothes the golden waters where
  The pearl fishers dive.

When she wept and begged a kiss
  Very close I'd hold her,
Oh I know so well in this
  Fine, fierce joy of memory
She was very young like me
  Tho' half an aeon older.

Once she kissed me very long,
  Tip-toed out the door,
Left me, took her light along,
  Faded as a music fades . . .
  Then I saw the changing shades,
  Color-blind no more.

LOUISE BOGAN (1897–1970)

Men Loved Wholly Beyond Wisdom

Men loved wholly beyond wisdom
Have the staff without the banner.
Like a fire in a dry thicket,
Rising within women's eyes
Is the love men must return.
Heart, so subtle now, and trembling,
What a marvel to be wise,
To love never in this manner!
To be quiet in the fern
Like a thing gone dead and still,
Listening to the prisoned cricket
Shake its terrible, dissembling
Music in the granite hill.

LANGSTON HUGHES (1902–1967)

Juke Box Love Song

I could take the Harlem night
and wrap around you,
Take the neon lights and make a crown,
Take the Lenox Avenue busses,
Taxis, subways,
And for your love song tone their rumble down.
Take Harlem's heartbeat,
Make a drumbeat,
Put it on a record, let it whirl,
And while we listen to it play,
Dance with you till day—
Dance with you, my sweet
  brown Harlem girl.

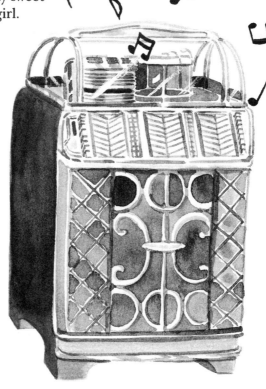

I Never Even Suggested It

I know lots of men who are in love and lots of men who
    are married and lots of men who are both,
And to fall out with their loved ones is what all of them
    are most loth.
They are conciliatory at every opportunity,
Because all they want is serenity and a certain amount
    of impunity.
Yes, many the swain who has finally admitted that the
    earth is flat
Simply to sidestep a spat,
Many the masculine Positively or Absolutely which has
    been diluted to an If
Simply to avert a tiff,
Many the two-fisted executive whose domestic conversation
    is limited to a tactfully interpolated Yes,
And then he is amazed to find that he is being raked
    backwards over a bed of coals nevertheless.
These misguided fellows are under the impression that
    it takes two to make a quarrel, that you can sidestep
    a crisis by nonaggression and nonresistance,
Instead of removing yourself to a discreet distance.
Passivity can be a provoking *modus operandi*;
Consider the Empire and Gandhi.
Silence is golden, but sometimes invisibility is golder.
Because loved ones may not be able to make bricks
    without straw but often they don't need any straw
    to manufacture a bone to pick or blood in their eye
    or a chip for their soft white shoulder.
It is my duty, gentlemen, to inform you that women are
    dictators all, and I recommend to you this moral:
In real life it takes only one to make a quarrel.

If This Be Love

If this be love, then let me leap
Into the abstract austerity,
Into the abysm where I peep
Shuddering with temerity,
O the unearthly loyalty,

Till the cold trees silver
Smoothly to a patine touched
And afternoon, like a golden bee,
Pulls, unwinds the spooled eyes;
Hold, hold in body's brace
Her curved shining, thus destroy
The virgin ecstasy of her face,
Contaminate with experience
The ghostly praise and young
Of her full wisdom sung.

And a cone of love around the honey
Comes; but the bee cuts there.

If it could be triumphant
No cruelty could be kinder:
It is sheer world all sunny
And time's out of his dry lair;
So high then is rapture higher,
Being compounded of this pain,
That the icy pinnacles of desire
Melt, and fires of blood congeal,
Till all's the quality of the real.
If this be love! O I remember
Tempest, and abysm gone.

It is that Bane of Self in Love

It is that bane of self in love
When all should be of love's self the dove,
That perfect creature's constant balm,
That is, a wholesome ball of calm.

But since we fought, we tore our skins,
Each raving in an ecstasy.
Thus thought love's world we had gone in,
Who had gone but in a storm'd sea.

'Twere to have been equal we hoped.
But hope too much, not love enough,
Made two who on a straw have groped;
Hands, tumid, closed on chaos' stuff.

Nor can we prove that human love
More solid is than thought's empire.
Since of the other each was above,
Under, was only ideas' fire.

Love is but warm simplicity.
It wants no divinity,
That clothes our human life in clothes,
Curled, rolled, woven, lover.

THEODORE ROETHKE (1908–1963)

The Voice

One feather is a bird,
I claim; one tree, a wood;
In her low voice I heard
More than a mortal should;
And so I stood apart,
Hidden in my own heart.

And yet I roamed out where
Those notes went, like the bird,
Whose thin song hung in air,
Diminished, yet still heard:
I lived with open sound,
Aloft, and on the ground.

That ghost was my own choice,
The shy cerulean bird;
It sang with her true voice,
And it was I who heard
A slight voice reply;
I heard; and only I.

Desire exults the ear:
Bird, girl, and ghostly tree,
The earth, the solid air—
Their slow song sang in me;
The long noon pulsed away,
Like any summer day.

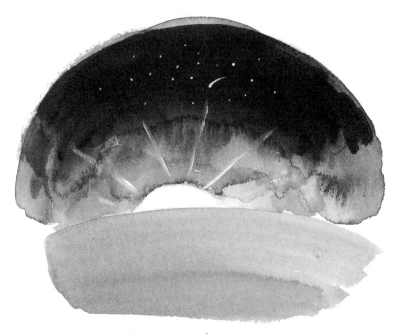

KENNETH PATCHEN (1911–1972)

Fall of the Evening Star

Speak softly; sun going down
Out of sight. Come near me now.

Dear dying fall of wings as birds
Complain against the gathering dark . . .

Exaggerate the green blood in grass;
The music of leaves scraping space;

Multiply the stillness by one sound;
By one syllable of your name . . .

And all that is little is soon giant,
All that is rare grows in common beauty

To rest with my mouth on your mouth
As somewhere a star falls

And the earth takes it softly, in natural love . . .
Exactly as we take each other . . . and go to sleep

Insomnia

The moon in the bureau mirror
looks out a million miles
(and perhaps with pride, at herself,
but she never, never smiles)
far and away beyond sleep, or
perhaps she's a daytime sleeper.

By the Universe deserted,
she'd tell it to go to hell,
and she'd find a body of water,
or a mirror, on which to dwell.
So wrap up care in a cobweb
and drop it down the well

into that world inverted
where left is always right,
where the shadows are really the body,
where we stay awake all night,
where the heavens are
    shallow as the sea
is now deep, and you
    love me.

Letter to N.Y.

In your next letter I wish you'd say
Where you are going and what you are doing:
How are the plays, and after the plays,
What other pleasures you're pursuing.

Taking cabs in the middle of the night,
Driving as if to save your soul
Where the road goes round and round the park
And the meter glares like a moral owl.

And the trees look so queer and green
Standing alone in big black caves,
And suddenly you're in a different place
Where everything seems to happen in waves.

And most of the jokes you just can't catch,
Like dirty words rubbed off a slate,
And the songs are loud but somewhat dim
And it gets so terribly late.

And coming out of the brownstone houses
To the gray sidewalk, the watered street,
One side of the buildings rise with the sun
Like a glistening field of wheat.

Wheat, not oats, dear. I'm afraid
If it's wheat, it's none of your sowing.
Nevertheless I'd like to know
What you are doing and where you are going.

Ah When You Drift

Ah when you drift hover before you kiss
More my mouth yours now, lips grow more to mine
Teeth click, suddenly your tongue like a mulled wine
Slides fire,—I wonder what the point of life is.
Do, down this night when I adore you, Lise,
So I forsake the blest assistant shine
Of deep-laid maps I made for summits, swine-
enchanted lover, loafing in the abyss?

Loaf hardly, while my nerves dance, while the gale
Moans like your hair down here. But I lie still,
Strengthless and smiling under a maenad rule.
Whose limbs worked once, whose imagination's grail
Many or some would nourish, must now I fill
My strength with desire, my cup with your tongue,
   no more Melpomene's, but Erato's fool? . . .

JOHN BERRYMAN

Your Shining

Your shining—where?—rays my wide room with gold;
Grey rooms all day, green streets I visited,
Blazed with you possible; other voices bred
Yours in my quick ear; when the rain was cold
Shiver it might make shoulders I behold
Sloping through kite-slipt hours, tingling. I said
A month since, 'I will see that cloud-gold head,
Those eyes lighten, and go by': then your thunder rolled.

Drowned all sound else, I come driven to learn
Fearful and happy, deafening rumours of
The complete conversations of the angels, now
As nude upon some warm lawn softly turn
Toward me the silences of your breasts . . . My vow! . . .
One knee unnerves the voyeur sky enough.

JOHN CIARDI (1916–1985)

To Judith Asleep

My dear, darkened in sleep, turned from the moon
That riots on curtain-stir with every breeze
Leaping in moths of light across your back . . .
Far off, then soft and sudden as petals shower
Down from wired roses—silently, all at once—
You turn, abandoned and naked, all let down
In ferny streams of sleep and petaled thighs
Rippling into my flesh's buzzing garden.

Far and familiar your body's myth-map lights,
Traveled by moon and dapple. Sagas were curved
Like scimitars to your hips. The raiders' ships
All sailed to your one port. And watchfires burned
Your image on the hills. Sweetly you drown
Male centuries in your chiaroscuro tide
Of breast and breath. All all my memory's shores
You frighten perfectly, washed familiar and far.

Ritual wars have climbed your shadowed flank
Where bravos dreaming of fair women tore
Rock out of rock to have your cities down
In loot of hearths and trophies of desire.
And desert monks have fought your image back
In a hysteria of mad skeletons.
Bravo and monk (the heads and tails of love)
I stand, a spinning coin of wish and dread,

Counting our life, our chairs, our books and walls,
Our clock whose radium eye and insect voice
Owns all our light and shade, and your white shell
Spiraled in moonlight on the bed's white beach;
Thinking, I might press you to my ear
And all your coils fall out in sounds of surf
Washing away our chairs, our books and walls,
Our bed and wish, our ticking light and dark.

Child, child, and making legend of my wish
Fastened alive into your naked sprawl—
Stir once to stop my fear and miser's panic
That time shall have you last and legendry
Undress to old bones from its moon brocade.
Yet sleep and keep our prime of time alive
Before that death of legend. My dear of all

Saga and century, sleep in familiar-far.
Time still must tick *this is, I am, we are.*

Frankie and Johnny

Frankie and Johnny were lovers,
Lordy, how they could love,
Swore to be true to each other,
True as the stars above,
    He was her man, but he done her wrong.

Little Frankie was a good gal,
As everybody knows,
She did all the work around the house,
And pressed her Johnny's clothes,
    He was her man, but he done her wrong.

Johnny was a yeller man,
With coal black, curly hair,
Everyone up in St. Louis
Thought he was a millionaire,
    He was her man, but he done her wrong.

Frankie went down to the bar-room,
Called for a bottle of beer,
Says, "Looky here, Mister Bartender,
Has my lovin' Johnny been here?
    He is my man, and he's doin' me wrong."

"I will not tell you no story,
I will not tell you no lie,
Johnny left here about an hour ago,
With a gal named Nelly Bly,
    He is your man, and he's doing you wrong."

Little Frankie went down Broadway,
With her pistol in her hand,
Said, "Stand aside you chorus gals,
I'm lookin' for my man,
    He is my man, and he's doin' me wrong."

The first time she shot him, he staggered,
The next time she shot him, he fell,
The last time she shot, O Lawdy,
There was a new man's face in hell,
She shot her man, for doin' her wrong.

"Turn me over doctor,
Turn me over slow,
I got a bullet in my left hand side,
Great God, it's hurtin' me so.
I was her man, but I done her wrong."

It was a rubber-tyred buggy,
Decorated hack,
Took poor Johnny to the graveyard,
Brought little Frankie back,
He was her man, but he done her wrong.

It was not murder in the first degree,
It was not murder in the third.
A woman simply dropped her man
Like a hunter drops his bird,
She shot her man, for doin' her wrong.

The last time I saw Frankie,
She was sittin' in the 'lectric chair,
Waitin' to go and meet her God
With the sweat runnin' out of her hair,
She shot her man, for doin' her wrong.

Walked on down Broadway,
As far as I could see,
All I could hear was a two string bow
Playin' *"Nearer my God to thee,"*
He was her man, and he done her wrong.

love note I: surely

Surely you stay my certain own, you stay
My you. All honest, lofty as a cloud.
Surely I could come now and find you high,
As mine as you ever were; should not be awed.
Surely your word would pop as insolent
As always: "Why, of course I love you, dear."
Your gaze, surely, ungauzed as I could want.
Your touches, that never were careful, what they were.
Surely— But I am very off from that.
From surely. From indeed. From the decent arrow
That was my clean naïveté and my faith.
This morning men deliver wounds and death.
They will deliver death and wounds tomorrow.
And I doubt all. You. Or a violet.

love note II: flags

Still, it is dear defiance now to carry
Fair flags of you above my indignation,
Top, with a pretty glory and a merry
Softness, the scattered pound of my cold passion.
I pull you down my foxhole. Do you mind?
You burn in bits of saucy color then.
I let you flutter out against the pained
Volleys. Against my power crumpled and wan.
You, and the yellow pert exuberance
Of dandelion days, unmocking sun:
The blowing of clear wind in your gay hair;
Love changeful in you (like a music, or
Like a sweet mournfulness, or like a dance,
Or like the tender struggle of a fan).

A Lovely Love

Let it be alleys. Let it be a hall
Whose janitor javelins epithet and thought
To cheapen hyacinth darkness that we sought
And played we found, rot, make the petals fall.
Let it be stairways, and a splintery box
Where you have thrown me, scraped me with your kiss,
Have honed me, have released me after this
Cavern kindness, smiled away our shocks.
That is the birthright of our lovely love
In swaddling clothes. Not like that Other one.
Not lit by any fondling star above.
Not found by any wise men, either. Run.
People are coming. They must not catch us here
Definitionless in this strict atmosphere.

JAMES BALDWIN (1924–1987)

A lady like landscapes

(FOR SIMONE SIGNORET)

A lady like landscapes,
wearing time like an amusing shawl
thrown over her shoulders
by a friend at the bazaar:

Every once in a while she turns in it
just like a little girl,
this way and that way:

Regarde.
Ça n'était pas donné bien sûr
mais c'est quand même beau, non?

Oui, Oui.
Et toi aussi.
Ou plutôt belle
since you are a lady.

It is impossible to tell
how beautiful, how real, unanswerable,
becomes your landscape as you move in it,
how beautiful the shawl.

Remembrance

for Paul

Your hands easy
weight, teasing the bees
hived in my hair, your smile at the
slope of my cheek. On the
occasion, you press
above me, glowing, spouting
readiness, mystery rapes
my reason.

When you have withdrawn
your self and the magic, when
only the smell of your
love lingers between
my breasts, then, only
then, can I greedily consume
your presence.

Refusal

Beloved,
In what other lives or lands
Have I known your lips
Your hands
Your laughter brave
Irreverent.
Those sweet excesses that
I do adore.
What surety is there
That we will meet again,
On other worlds some
Future time undated.
I defy my body's haste.
Without the Promise
Of one more sweet encounter
I will not deign to die.

SYLVIA PLATH (1932–1963)

Love Letter

Not easy to state the change you made.
If I'm alive now, then I was dead,
Though, like a stone, unbothered by it,
Staying put according to habit.
You didn't just toe me an inch, no—
Nor leave me to set my small bald eye
Skyward again, without hope, of course,
Of apprehending blueness, or stars.

That wasn't it. I slept, say: a snake
Masked among black rocks as a black rock
In the white hiatus of winter—
Like my neighbours, taking no pleasure
In the million perfectly-chiselled
Cheeks alighting each moment to melt
My cheek of basalt. They turned to tears,
Angels weeping over dull natures,
But didn't convince me. Those tears froze.
Each dead head had a visor of ice.

And I slept on like a bent finger.
The first thing I saw was sheer air
And the locked drops rising in a dew
Limpid as spirits. Many stones lay
Dense and expressionless round about.
I didn't know what to make of it.
I shone, mica-scaled, and unfolded
To pour myself out like a fluid
Among bird feet and the stems of plants.
I wasn't fooled. I knew you at once.

Tree and stone glittered, without shadows.
My finger-length grew lucent as glass.
I started to bud like a March twig:
An arm and a leg, an arm, a leg.
From stone to cloud, so I ascended.
Now I resembled a sort of god
Floating through the air in my soul-shift
Pure as a pane of ice. It's a gift.

Anne Bradstreet (1612?–1672): English-born poet who lived in the Massachusetts Bay Colony. Her lyrics address domestic life, religious piety, and family relationships, and are characterized by a tenderness and beauty not common in other Puritan writings. Bradstreet's *The Tenth Muse Lately Sprung Up in America* is the first volume of original verse to be published in America, and the only one to be published in her lifetime. Her other works include *Religious Experiences*, an autobiographical piece, and *Meditations, Divine and Moral*, a collection of aphorisms.

Phillis Wheatley (1753?–1784): African-born American poet and first black woman writer in the U.S. Wheatley came to Boston as a slave and was given an education. She was famous as a poet in her day and was received in London's aristocratic circles.

George Moses Horton (1797?–1883?): Known as the "Colored Bard of North Carolina," Horton was the first Southern black man to publish a volume of poetry in America. Born a slave, Horton taught himself to read and made weekend trips to the University of North Carolina at Chapel Hill, where he sold love lyrics to students, who in turn loaned him books. He lived and worked as a poet, publishing his poems and antislavery periodicals, in Chapel Hill, for over thirty years until Emancipation. He later settled and died in Philadelphia.

Ralph Waldo Emerson (1803–1882): New England poet, essayist and philosopher who became the chief proponent of the American literary and philosophic movement, Transcendentalism. This movement rejected scientific rationalism and espoused intuition as the only way to comprehend reality in the world, where every fact of nature represents a spiritual truth. Emerson's prose style is poetic, with an instinctive rather than logical form, and characterized by recurrent images and themes. His poetry, however, is often regarded as severe and didactic.

Edgar Allan Poe (1809–1849): Poet, critic and short story writer born in Boston. Several of his stories, including "The Tell-Tale Heart" (1843), "The Murders in the Rue Morgue" (1841) and "The Purloined Letter" (1841), established him as a master of the macabre and the principal progenitor of the detective story.

Walt Whitman (1819–1892): Poet, journalist and essayist born in Long Island. His significant works include *Leaves of Grass* (1855), and poems, "When Lilacs Last in the Dooryard Bloom'd" (an elegy for Abraham Lincoln), "Song of Myself," and "Crossing Brooklyn Ferry." He was known as the "bard of democracy," and his poetry addresses the importance of the self, the equality of all people, comradeship and timelessness of the soul.

Emily Dickinson (1830–1886): Born in Amherst, Massachusetts, Dickinson led a rather secluded life and was dominated by her father, a stern Calvinist. She wrote poetry throughout her adult life, although only a handful of her two thousand poems were published in her lifetime. Her concise verses, usually consisting of four-line stanzas with simple meter schemes, contain a wealth of emotions.

Thomas Bailey Aldrich (1836–1907): New Hampshire poet, editor, novelist and playwright. After serving as a journalist and war correspondent, Aldrich became editor of the *Atlantic Monthly* (1881–1900). His popular works include *The Stillwater Tragedy* (1880) and *The Story of a Bad Boy* (1870).

Theodore Dreiser (1871–1945): Known principally as a novelist, Dreiser was a leading exponent of American Naturalism. His most famous works include *Sister Carrie* (1900) and *An American Tragedy* (1925). Dreiser's novels were considered amoral in his time, but his chief theme was really the conflict between human needs and the demands of society for material success.

Robert Frost (1874–1963): Poet best known for his verses dealing with New England life and character. Unlike most modern poets, Frost was a simple, moral poet who celebrated rural, democratic joys and nature. He wrote in traditional verse forms, but he is known especially for the tension of thought and feeling, and the tension between traditional meter and colloquial speech in his verse. His famous poems include "The Road Not Taken" and "Stopping by Woods on a Snowy Evening."

Carl Sandburg (1878–1967): Poet influenced by Walt Whitman and known for his free verse poems about agricultural and industrial America, American landscape, geography and history, including historical figures and common people. Among his celebrated works are *Smoke and Steel* (1920), the four-volume *Abraham Lincoln*, of which the second part won him the Pulitzer Prize, and *The American Songbag* (1927).

Wallace Stevens (1879–1955): Critically recognized as one of the most influential poets of the 20th century, Stevens did not receive widespread acclaim until the publication of his *Collected Poems* (1954, Pulitzer Prize). His work is characterized by the idea that the imagination constructs order, understanding and knowledge in a world lacking perceptible spiritual meaning. His famous poems include "The Emperor of Ice Cream," "Sunday Morning," and "Le Monocle de Mon Oncle" among others.

William Carlos Williams (1883–1963): Poet, essayist, playwright and novelist who was also a medical doctor in Rutherford, New Jersey, the "Paterson" of his poems. Williams' poetry addresses the details and issues of every day life in America, and concentrates upon the familiar and local. By abandoning complicated rhyme schemes and subjects, he strove to make his verse accessible to all readers. His works of poetry include *Collected Poems* (1934), *Collected Later Poems* (1950), *Collected Earlier Poems* (1951), *Pictures from Brueghel and Other Poems* (1963, Pulitzer Prize) and the five-volume epic *Paterson* (1963).

Sara Teasdale (1884–1933): Known for the intensity of her verses, Teasdale was associated with Harriet Monroe's literary group in Chicago. She received a Pulitzer Prize for her *Love Songs* (1917); other significant works include *Sonnets to Duse and Other Poems* (1907), *Rivers to the Sea* (1915), *Dark of the Moon* (1926), and *Strange Victory* (1933). Teasdale committed suicide in 1933.

Elinor Wylie (1885–1928): Poet and novelist known for the precise yet colorful imagery of her verses, and the astute analysis of emotion in her love poems. Her poetry volumes include *Nets to Catch the Wind* (1921), *Trivial Breath* (1928), and *Collected Poems* (1932). Her historical novels include *Jennifer Lorn* (1923), *The Venetian Glass Nephew* (1925), and *The Orphan Angel* (1926).

Ezra Pound (1885–1972): Poet, editor and critic who became one of the most influential and controversial figures in modern literature. Born in Idaho of a New England family, Pound eventually went to live in England and Italy. Pound is known as the guiding spirit of Imagism, a poetic movement which emphasizes examining an object directly without use of unnecessary rhetoric, free verses rather than forced meter, and purity of image and metaphor. As an editor, Pound found publishers for the early works of then unknown writers like T.S. Eliot, Wyndham Lewis, James Joyce, William Carlos Williams, Ernest Hemingway and Marianne Moore.

Robinson Jeffers (1887–1962): Son of a Presbyterian minister, Jeffers was heavily influenced by classical and biblical sources. Many of his poems and the imagery within them is based on the Carmel/Big Sur region of California. Jeffers' poetry juxtaposes the dismal, isolated condition of modern man with the striking, rugged beauty of the landscape. He was sometimes mistakenly regarded as nihilist because he was strongly influenced by Nietzche's ideas of individualism, although his poetry acknowledges the existence of God, but a God who has forsaken humanity. His well-known works include *Tamar, And Other Poems* (1924), *The Tower Beyond Tragedy* (1924), and *Thurso's Landing* (1932).

John Crowe Ransom (1888–1974): Poet and critic who attended and taught at Vanderbilt University, where he was a key member of The Fugitives, a literary group that espoused political conservatism, and supported the southern agrarian ideal. Their poetry reaffirmed formal classicism and ignored such freer movements as Imagism. Much of Ransom's work sought to prove that humanity can become spiritually and physically intact only in a traditional, rural society like the antebellum South. Ransom's spare, classic style is marked by irony and realism, and the theme of decay—of the individual, society and values. Ransom's poetry volumes include *Chills and Fever* (1924), *Two Gentlemen in Bonds* (1927), and *Selected Poems* (1945; rev 1963, 1969).

Conrad Aiken (1889–1973): Writer whose childhood tragedy (Aiken's father killed his wife and then himself when the poet was a young boy) led to an intense interest in psychoanalysis and the development of identity. Aiken's poetry is characterized by his use of the forms and sounds of music; volumes include *The Jig of Forslin* (1916), *The Charnel Rose* (1918), *Selected Poems* (1929; Pulitzer Prize, 1930), *Brownstone Ecologues* (1942), *The Kid* (1947), and *Collected Poems, 1916–1970*. Aiken's fiction is laden with symbolism and characterized by his mastery of interior monologue.

Edna St. Vincent Millay (1892–1950): Poet and Vassar graduate who lived in and wrote about Greenwich Village. The poetry she wrote during the 1920s, celebrates Bohemian life, love and moral freedom with a fresh, lyrical joyfulness. Influenced by the Elizabethan poets and Keats, Millay used conventional forms in a flexible style and was noted for her sonnets. Her works include *A Few Figs from Thistles* (1920), *The Harp Weaver and Other Poems* (1923) for which she won the Pulitzer Prize, *The Buck in the Snow* (1928), *Fatal Interview* (1931) and *Conversation at Midnight* (1937).

Dorothy Parker (1893–1967): Poet, short story writer and essayist known for her biting wit and sardonic verses. She was the drama critic for *Vanity Fair* and book reviewer for *The New Yorker.* Her poems are usually cynical but elegant commentaries on fading or faded love.

E.E. Cummings (1894–1962): Poet, critic, novelist and painter born in Cambridge, Massachusetts and educated at Harvard. One of the most gifted and innovative poets of his time, Cummings is known for his eccentric use of punctuation and typography to highlight rhythm patterns. He is also known for using dialect, slang and the rhythms of jazz in his works. Cummings' poems include love poems, celebrations of sex, witty character sketches and satires about the institutions of his time. Cummings wrote 16 volumes of poetry, including *Tulips and Chimneys* (1923), *ViVa* (1931), *50 Poems* (1940), *1 x 1* (1944) and *The Complete Poems 1913–1962* (1972). Until the 1930s, he preferred the lowercase e. e. cummings.

Mark Van Doren (1894–1972): Poet, critic and novelist who taught at Columbia University (1920–1959) and served as an editor and critic for the *Nation* in the 1920s and 1930s. Van Doren's contemplative verse is strongly influenced by the English romantic poets, Wordsworth in particular. He was a versatile writer, but his poetry collections include *Collected Poems 1922–1938I* (winner of the 1939 Pulitzer Prize); *That Shining Place* (1969), and *Good Morning* (1973).

Elizabeth Bishop (1911–1979): Poet whose first volume of poetry was *North and South* (1946), which she later reissued with *A Cold Spring* in 1955 to win the 1956 Pulitzer Prize for poetry. Bishop traveled frequently, living around the world and eventually settling in Brazil. Her poetry is very descriptive, with a simple but subtly tender style.

Gwendolyn Brooks (B. 1917): One of the foremost black American poets of the mid-20th century, Brooks' poems address the language, struggles and dreams of American blacks, particularly those of her native Chicago. She received the Pulitzer Prize for poetry in 1950 for *Annie Allen* (1949), and later published *In the Mecca* (1968), *Family Pictures* (1970), *Beckonings* (1975), *Primer for Blacks* (1980), and *To Disembark* (1981) among other works.

James Baldwin (1924–1987): Novelist, essayist and poet best known for his novels *Go Tell It on the Mountain* (1953) and *Giovanni's Room* (1956), moving accounts of black men's spiritual, sexual and emotional struggles. Baldwin's essays are passionate attacks on institutionalized racial discrimination in America before Civil Rights reform. As a protest against the inhumane conditions American blacks faced, Baldwin left the U.S. and moved to France at the age of twenty-four.

Maya Angelou (B. 1928): Poet, novelist and entertainer best known for her portrayals of strong African-American women. Her works celebrate the black experience, as well as the capacity to survive and triumph over adversity. Her autobiographical novels include *I Know Why the Caged Bird Sings* (1970), *Gather Together in my Name* (1974) and *The Heart of a Woman* (1981), which chronicle her harsh experiences of growing up in Arkansas, being raped at the age of seven and bearing a child at the age of sixteen. Her celebrated books of poetry include *And Still I Rise* (1978), *Shaker, Why Don't You Sing?* (1983), and *Phenomenal Woman* (1994).

Sylvia Plath (1932–1963): Poet and novelist whose prolifically creative but brief, tragic life was marked by her struggle with schizophrenia and suicidal tendencies. In 1955 Plath received a Fulbright fellowship to England, where she met and married poet Ted Hughes. Her works of poetry include *The Colossus* (1960), and posthumous publications *Ariel* (1965), *Crossing the Water* (1971), *Winter Trees* (1972), and *The Collected Poems* (1981), edited by Ted Hughes and winner of a Pulitzer Prize. The poems written shortly before she took her life in 1963 are characterized by their graphic morbidity, honesty, ironic wit and stylistic definition.

Love Poetry from Hippocrene . . .

Classic American Love Poems
Hardcover: 135 pages • 6 x 9 • illustrations • 0-7818-0645-3 • W •
$17.50hc • (731)
Paperback: 135 pages • 6 x 9 • illustrations • 0-7818-0894-4 • W •
$12.95pb • (266)

Classic English Love Poems
   This romantic anthology contains 87 classic poems of love from 48 poets who have continued to inspire over the years. The charmingly illustrated collection includes the timeless love lyrics of Geoffrey Chaucer, Sir Philip Sidney, William Shakespeare, Ben Jonson, John Donne, Robert Herrick, Andrew Marvell, Aphra Behn, John Dryden, Alexander Pope, Lady Mary Montagu, John Keats, Percy Bysshe Shelley, Lord Byron, William Wordsworth, Elizabeth Barrett Browning, Emily Brontë, Christina Rossetti, Thomas Hardy and Gerard Manley Hopkins among others.
Hardcover: 143 pages • 6 x 9 • illustrations • 0-7818-0572-4 • W •
$17.50hc • (671)
Paperback: 143 pages • 6 x 9 • illustrations • 0-7818-0895-2 • W •
$12.95pb • (283)

Classic French Love Poems
Edited by Lisa Neal
   This volume contains over 25 beautiful illustrations by famous artist Maurice Leloir and 120 inspiring poems translated into English from French, the language of love itself.
130 pages • 6 x 9 • illustrations • 0-7818-0573-2 • W • $17.50hc • (672)

Hebrew Love Poems
Edited by David C. Gross
   Includes 90 love lyrics from biblical times to modern day, with illustrations by Shagra Weil.
91 pages • 6 x 9 • illustrations • 0-7818-0430-2 • W • $14.95pb • (473)

Irish Love Poems: Dánta Grá

Edited by Paula Redes

This striking collection includes illustrations by Peadar McDaid and poems that span four centuries up to the most modern of poets, Nuala Ni Dhomhnaill, Brendan Kennedy, and Nobel Prize winner, Seamus Heaney.

146 pages • 6 x 9 • illustrations • 0-7818-0396-9 • W • $17.50hc • (70)

Scottish Love Poems: A Personal Anthology

Edited by Lady Antonia Fraser

Lady Fraser collects the loves and passions of her fellow Scots, from Burns to Aileen Campbell Nye, into a book that will find a way to touch everyone's heart.

253 pages • 5 ½ x 8 ½ • 0-7818-0406-X • NA • $14.95pb • (482)

Longing for a Kiss: Love Poems from Many Lands

This unique anthology contains over 100 love poems from around the world—each one on the all-important subject of the kiss.

197 pages • 6 x 9 • illustrations • 0-7818-0671-2 • W • $19.95hc • (769)

Love Poems from Around the World

From one corner of the globe to the other—and among the diverse countries, cultures and peoples in between—one thing will always remain universal: the powerful grasp of love. This charming, extensive collection of over 450 poems from around the world celebrates love in all of its unique facets. From the countrysides of Ireland to the city streets of China, the reader is swept away on an amazing cross-cultural journey through lost love, love's follies, love's strength, unrequited love, and love attained.

Includes poems from such internationally-renowned, classic poets as William Carlos Williams, Gwendolyn Brooks, Christina Rossetti, James Joyce, Dante Alighieri, Judah Halevi, Wen I-to, Adam Mickiewicz, Sappho, and the Kamasutra of Vatsyayana, among others. The collection is arranged alphabetically by country.

416 pages • 6 x 9 • 0-7818-0752-2 • W • $14.95pb • (525)

Treasury of Wedding Poems, Quotations & Short Stories

Compiled by the Editors of Hippocrene Books
Illustrated by Rosemary Fox

This beautifully illustrated volume contains over 100 poems, quotations and short stories from over 50 authors—all on the subject of weddings!

142 pages • 6 x 9 • illustrations • 0-7818-0636-4 • W • $17.50hc • (729)

Proverbs and Quotations from Hippocrene Books . . .

Treasury of Love Proverbs from Many Lands

This anthology includes more than 600 proverbs on love from over 50 languages and cultures, addressing such timeless experiences as first love, unrequited love, jealousy, marriage, flirtation and attraction.

146 pages • 6 x 9 • illustrations • 0-7818-0563-5 • W • $17.50hc • (698)

Treasury of Love Quotations from Many Lands

This charming gift volume contains over 500 quotations from over 400 great writers, thinkers and personalities—all on the subject of love. These are words of wit and wisdom from all over the world (over 40 countries and languages), from antiquity to present day. With lovely illustrations throughout, this volume is the perfect gift of love for anyone.

144 pages • 6 x 9 • illustrations • 0-7818-0574-0 • W • $17.50hc • (673)

African Proverbs
Compiled by Gerd de Ley

This extensive collection of 1,755 proverbs spans all regions of the African continent, revealing much about the wisdom, humor, and character of its people and cultures. Each proverb is arranged alphabetically by key word and includes the country, province, or tribe of origin.

124 pages • 6 x 9 • illustrations • 0-7818-0691-7 • W • $17.50hc • (778)

American Proverbs
compiled by Judith Reitman
illustrated by Barbara Smolover

Americans are a practical people, and they have a gift for coining pithy phrases. Much of the wit and wisdom commonly attributed to other cultures has, in fact, had its origin in America—in the cornfields, coal mines, timberlands, and on the reservations and city streets of yesteryear. This collection of over 150 proverbs captures the colorful and diversified ways Americans uniquely express their views of life. Proverbs are arranged by topic: Body & Mind, Friendship & Family, Men & Women, Money, The Spirit, African American & Native American Proverbs, and State-Specific Proverbs. Exquisite illustrations throughout.

107 pages • 5½ x 8¼ • 25 b/w illustrations • $14.95hc • 0-7818-0753-0 • W • (414)

Arabic Proverbs
Joseph Hanki

First published in Egypt in 1897, this collection contains 600 Arabic proverbs written in colloquial Arabic with side-by-side English translations; where appropriate, explanations are given of the custom which gave rise to the proverb. Many of these proverbs show a recognizable Biblical influence and are of great historical interest. Attractive, fascinating, and enjoyable, this book as many roles: reference guide, learning tool, and treasury of ethnic heritage.
144 pages • 6 x 9 • 0-7818-0631-3 • W • $11.95pb • (711)

Irish Proverbs
Compiled by the Editors of Hippocrene Books
Illustrated by Fergus Lyons

In the great oral tradition of Ireland, sharp-witted proverbs have been passed on for generations. This collection of over 200 proverbs recalls the experiences of Irish men and women in the cities, in the country, and by the sea. County Sligo native Fergus Lyons adds style and humor with clever illustrations.
104 pages • 6 x 9 • 35 b/w illustrations • 0-7818-0676-3 • W • $14.95hc • (761)

Scottish Proverbs
Compiled by the Editors of Hippocrene Books
Illustrated by Shona Grant

Through opinions on love, drinking, work, money, law and politics, the sharp wit and critical eye of the Scottish spirit is strikingly conveyed in this collection. Glasgow artist Shona Grant illustrates the collection with 30 clever drawings.
107 pages • 6 x 9 • 30 b/w illustrations • 0-7818-0648-8 • W • $14.95hc • (719)

International Dictionary of Proverbs
Gerd de Ley

This comprehensive dictionary is a dynamic collection of 8,000 proverbs gathered from over 300 countries and regions. There is nothing in print today which resembles this reference dictionary's global scope and complete subject coverage. The proverbs are arranged alphabetically by country, and an index listing 2,000 key words is also provided. Gerd de Ley is an internationally-known author of reference books.
Hardcover: 437 pages • 5 ½ x 8 ½ • 0-7818-0620-8 • NA • $29.50hc • (706)
Paperback: 437 pages • 5 ½ x 8 ½ • 0-7818-0531-7 • NA • $19.95pb • (656)

All prices subject to change without prior notice. To purchase Hippocrene Books contact your local bookstore, call (718) 454-2366, or write to: HIPPOCRENE BOOKS, 171 Madison Avenue, New York, NY 10016. Please enclose check or money order, adding $5.00 shipping (UPS) for the first book and $.50 for each additional book.